THE SECOND BRIDGE

Building Lasting Love
A Practical Guide to Love, Marriage, and Family

What 225 respondents and two very different marriages
taught me about building lasting love

By
ABAS ALHASSAN

THE SECOND BRIDGE: Building Lasting Love
A Practical Guide to Relationship, Love, Marriage, and Family

Published in Johannesburg, South Africa
First Edition: 2026

ISBN: 978-1-0492-6826-2

DEDICATION

TABLE OF CONTENTS

FOREWORD

Bridging Love, Culture, and Conscious Choice

By Dr Bàbá Amani Olúbánjọ Buntu
Transformation Strategist, Community Scholar and
Therapist

The Second Bridge: Building Lasting Love is a thoughtful and timely contribution to ongoing conversations about how women and men can sustain meaningful and enduring relationships. The book is grounded in candid self-reflection and cross-cultural inquiry, and it benefits from the author's willingness to place his own life journey at the centre of the narrative. His experiences—from growing up in a polygamous household, to building a transatlantic professional career, to navigating two very different marriages—provide an authentic and credible lens through which relational principles are explored. This personal grounding gives the book a sense of honesty and accessibility that many readers will find relatable.

What sets The Second Bridge apart is its deliberate effort to connect not only geographical contexts but also relational worldviews. By drawing insights from African settings alongside Western perspectives, the book challenges narrow or monolithic understandings of marriage. It demonstrates that while the core needs of trust, appreciation, and respect may be shared, the ways in which these needs are expressed are shaped by cultural, social, and historical conditions. This comparative approach strengthens the book's relevance and ensures that it speaks to diverse audiences. At the same time, the emphasis on dignity, community, and relational harmony reflects values that are deeply rooted in African traditions.

The metaphor of the "bridge" carries particular significance in African epistemology, and the author uses it effectively to frame his reflections on marriage. In many African cultures, the bridge symbolizes connection, passage, and resilience. Among the AmaZulu, marriage is likened to building a bridge between generations and clans, affirming the communal dimension of union. Akan wisdom reminds us that "the river may be wide, but the bridge makes it crossable," highlighting how shared vision and commitment enable couples to overcome challenges. Yorùbá philosophy understands the bridge as a conduit of Àṣẹ—the life force that enables movement and transformation—flowing between partners. Within this framing, marriage becomes a conscious act of balance, mutual respect, and intentional construction.

Although the book is written for both women and men, it is significant that it is voiced from the perspective of an African man. Men's experiences of marriage, separation, and emotional struggle are often less openly explored, particularly when they involve vulnerability and self-examination. The author's humility and willingness to introspect provide an important reminder of the role of emotional intelligence in sustaining relationships. His reflections are grounded in lived experience, making the book both practical and accessible.

In a time when many people are skeptical about marriage—fatigued by stories of broken unions and uncertain about its relevance—The Second Bridge offers hope. It provides practical guidance for those who may feel they have lost direction, while also challenging the assumption that marriage exists solely to meet family or societal expectations. The book insists that marriage must be meaningful, life-giving, and strengthening to those within it. This is an important intervention, particularly within African contexts often marked by tensions between tradition and modernity.

Overall, The Second Bridge is a hopeful, reflective, and action-oriented work. It invites readers to approach love with intentionality, self-awareness, and respect for both personal and communal well-being. It speaks to the realities of marriage in our time while affirming enduring values that can help women and men build strong and sustainable families.

INTRODUCTION: THE JOURNEY BEGINS

*What can a man raised in a Nigerian polygamous
household, who navigated a 35-year marriage across three
countries, experienced divorce at 60, and then built a thriving
second marriage teach us about relationships? Everything.*

A Story of Two Marriages

I sat in my leadership coaching office in Sandton, Johannesburg, listening to yet another executive describe their struggling marriage. As they talked about communication breakdowns, growing apart, and feeling trapped in a relationship that no longer worked, something twisted in my chest. I knew exactly what they were experiencing. Not from my professional training. Not from textbooks or workshops. But from 35 years of living it myself.

The irony wasn't lost on me. Here I was, a Leadership and Executive Coach who helps others navigate complex personal and professional challenges, yet I couldn't save my own marriage. For years, I carried the weight of that failure silently, wondering if I had any right to guide others when my own relationship crumbled. It was then I realised the progress I had made as a coach. Being a professional coach gave me the clarity I needed to be able to make important decisions in my life including that of my marriage. An honour so many people might not have in their lifetime.

Then something shifted. At 61, fourteen months after my divorce was finalized, I met someone who would become my current wife. Within four months—after intentional courtship with marriage coaching—we married. Today, I'm experiencing a partnership I didn't know was possible. Not perfect, but healthy. Not without challenges, but with tools to navigate them. Not built on the mistakes of my past, but on the wisdom gained from them. This book is the result of both journeys—the one that ended and the one that's promising.

Where I Come From

I grew up in Nigeria in a polygamous household. My father had multiple wives, and I witnessed first-hand how complex family dynamics operate when traditions, culture, and multiple relationships intersect under one roof. Some days it worked remarkably well. Other days, the tension could be cut with a knife. This upbringing gave me insights most relationship experts never experience—the reality of shared resources, divided attention, sibling dynamics across different mothers, and the delicate balance of fairness in an inherently complicated structure.

At 25, I married through a family introduction. My wife and I had known each other for four years, but we had no relationship during that time. This is important to understand: we didn't date. We didn't court in the modern sense. We knew of each other, but we didn't know each other. This pattern—common in traditional African marriages—would shape the next 35 years of my life.

We built a life together across three countries—Nigeria, Ghana, and South Africa. We raised four children, who are now adults. We accumulated four grandchildren—two boys and two girls. From the outside, we likely looked successful. A growing family. Geographic mobility. Professional advancement through my career as an accountant, auditor, and eventually banker before transitioning to leadership and executive coaching. We checked the boxes society expects. But inside the marriage, we were struggling. We had never really known each other, and despite 35 years together, we never truly learned how.

Nineteen Years of Trying to Leave

Most people don't know this, but I tried to divorce four times over 19 years:

The first time, I went to a spiritual leader seeking permission to leave. But empathy for my wife, our young children, and societal negative views of divorce pulled me back. I stayed.

Second time the same year, I relocated to South Africa, I tried again. Same result. Empathy for her, concern for the children who still needed us and what the society will say about me. I stayed.

Third time the pattern repeated. The weight of responsibility, the fear of disrupting our children's lives, the cultural expectations—all conspired to keep me in the marriage. I stayed again.

The fourth time, something was different. Our children were grown and gone, building their own lives and at my age, societal views about my life didn't matter to me. I was approaching retirement, facing the prospect of spending my final decades or less in a relationship that had become more about avoidance than connection. We barely spoke. We maneuvered around each other in our own home. Seeing each other triggered panic attacks in us as she confessed to me before the divorce. The divorce was finalized exactly one year after filing when I was 60 years old.

There were clear signs of incompatibility from the beginning of the marriage. It felt more like a contest of superiority than a partnership. I applied logic to every decision that had to be made, which made negotiation impossible. I realised my mistake when she started applying the same logic which made compromise difficult.

We started on the wrong footing. There was no single moment when the marriage collapsed. No dramatic argument. No final betrayal that could be neatly named and blamed. What happen instead was quieter and far more damaging. Sometimes hours passed without a word exchanged. Not because there was nothing to say, but because saying anything felt risky. Every sentence carried the possibility of misunderstanding, defensiveness, or exhaustion. Silence became safer than connection.

What died first was curiosity. We stopped asking each other questions that mattered. What followed was emotional safety. And slowly, almost imperceptibly, the spirit of the marriage weakened, not through cruelty or neglect, but through the steady absence of engagement.

At the time, I did not have language for what was happening. I only knew that something essential was missing, and could not name it. Looking back now, I understand that this was not a failure of love alone, it was failure of communication, courage, and shared emotional skill. That silence did not end the marriage immediately. It allowed it to continue, hollowed out, and increasingly lonely.

The Truth Nobody Talks About

Here's what most relationship books won't tell you. Society conditions us to view divorce as failure, as something to be ashamed of, as evidence we didn't try hard enough. But after 35 years, four attempts to leave, multiple rounds of counselling from relations, friends, spiritual leaders and professionals that never quite addressed our core issues, and decades of trying to make it work—the end wasn't a failure. It was freedom.

We don't have a relationship now. We never really did. What we had was a partnership of obligation, cultural expectation, and shared responsibility for raising children. Those are important things. They kept us together for years. But they're not the same as genuine connection, mutual understanding, and the kind of companionship that makes marriage not just endurable but enjoyable.

I'm sharing this not to be harsh, but to be honest. Because somewhere, someone reading this is trapped in a similar situation, feeling guilty for wanting out, wondering if they're being selfish or impatient. You're not. Sometimes the bravest thing you can do is acknowledge what isn't working and make the hard choice to change it.

Fourteen Months of Transformation

Over the years during which I filed for divorce, I kept asking myself what I did wrong. I tried several ways to make the marriage work without success. After the divorce was finalized, I spent fourteen months processing, learning, and preparing. This wasn't idle time. I was actively working to understand what went wrong, what I wanted moving forward, and what truly matters in relationships.

As part of the process, I conducted comprehensive research— surveying 225 respondents from both the United States and Africa, conducting in-depth interviews, and analyzing what makes relationships work across cultures. The findings challenged some of the general believes about cultural differences in relationships. For example, despite vast cultural differences, couples' views about finance were remarkably similar as 80% of USA respondents and 75% of African respondents cited it as critical and, four out of the five African couples interviewed said money was important in their relationships (See Chapter 9).

But I also discovered what works. I learned that successful couples aren't those who never have problems—they're the ones who've developed tools to navigate challenges together. They communicate openly. They respect each other's individuality while building shared purpose. They understand that love alone isn't enough; you need compatibility, commitment, and consistent effort.

Fourteen months post-divorce, I had clarity. I knew what I wanted. I knew what I needed. I knew what I would not compromise on. I was ready.

Building Something Better

One day, a female friend who knew me called me to come immediately to meet someone whom she thought we could be compatible, I left everything I was doing to honour the invitation where I was introduced to my current wife. From our first conversation, it was different. Not the swept-away infatuation of youth, but something more substantial. Recognition. Compatibility. The sense of meeting someone who fit. It took me only one hour after our first conversation to come to that conclusion and the meeting lasted for less than two hours.

I had compiled my research. I had written about what matters in relationships. I had my checklist—not a superficial list of preferences, but core values, communication styles, life goals, and relationship expectations. She ticked all the boxes. Not because she was perfect, but because we were compatible.

We didn't rush, but we didn't waste time either. We engaged in intentional courtship. We did marriage coaching before getting married—addressing potential challenges, aligning expectations, building communication tools. Four months after meeting, we got married.

In my current marriage, we talk—really talk—every day. We understand what we're building: a companionship where both partners work, maintain individual identities, and choose to invest in the relationship daily. There's mutual respect. Active communication. The freedom to address issues before they become crises. It's not perfect, but it's healthy. And at 63, I finally understand what marriage can be when built on the right foundation.

Why I Wrote This Book

I'm not a relationship therapist with decades of academic credentials. I'm not a psychologist with clinical research. I'm a Leadership and Executive Coach who lived both failure and success in marriage. I'm someone who grew up seeing polygamy work and struggle. I'm someone who married without truly knowing my partner and spent 35 years paying the price. I'm someone who finally built what I should have had all along.

This book exists because I wish someone had been this honest with me from the beginning. I wish someone had explained that you need to understand what you want in a relationship and know your partner well before marriage, not just knowing them. I wish someone had validated that staying in a broken relationship isn't noble—it's slowly destructive. I wish someone had shown me that it's never too late to build something better.

So, I'm being that person for you. Not preaching from a pedestal of perfection, but sharing from the trenches of real experience—the failures that taught me what doesn't work and the success that's showing me what does.

What I share here is not offered as judgment—of myself, my former spouse, or anyone reading these words. It is shared with compassion for how difficult it can be to name painful truths, especially when silence once felt like survival. If parts of this story feel confronting, my hope is that they are received not as accusation, but as invitation—an invitation to reflect, to learn, and to heal at your own pace.

Many African marital traditions, including extended family involvement and polygamous structures, were not originally designed to diminish intimacy or agency. They emerged from contexts of survival, communal responsibility, lineage continuity, and shared labour. When these practices are discussed without their emotional and historical context, they risk being misunderstood—either romanticised or unfairly reduced to sources of harm.

Colonial and postcolonial systems did not only dispossess African communities of land and labour; they also disrupted inherited models of family, masculinity, authority, and emotional expression. Many African adults today carry expectations of provision without emotional language, authority without guidance, and responsibility without support. These historical fractures continue to influence how love, conflict, and silence are negotiated in modern relationships.

What Makes This Book Different

This book is written from a position that is still rarely articulated in conversations about love and marriage: that of an African man willing to examine failure publicly, to speak about divorce without bravado or blame, and to reflect on renewal without denying loss. My perspective is shaped by movement—between cultures, continents, belief systems, and relational models—and by the tension that movement creates.

African men are often expected to embody certainty—to lead, provide, and endure—while remaining largely silent about confusion, emotional loss, or relational regret. This silence does not mean absence of feeling; it often signals absence of permission. Part of the work of this book is to break that silence carefully, without spectacle, and with respect for the weight many men carry quietly.

1. Cross-Cultural Research

This book is among the few relationship guides grounded in original cross-continental data with original survey data from 225 respondents across two continents combined with the lived experience of an African man openly examining marital failure and renewal   .
The findings challenge assumptions and reveal universal truths that transcend cultural boundaries.

The research presented here does not stand apart from my story; it stands alongside it. Listening to voices from Africa and the United States forced me to confront where my personal experience was unique, where it was shared, and where cultural context shaped interpretation. This dialogue between lived experience and collective insight is what ultimately gave this book its direction.

2. Complete Honesty About Failure

Most relationship experts write from success. I write from both—35 years of struggle followed by a marriage that works. You'll get both the warnings and the solutions, the mistakes and the corrections.

3. Comprehensive Coverage

From choosing a partner to aging together, this book covers the complete relationship lifecycle. Most books focus on one stage. This guides you through all of them.

4. Practical Tools

Some chapters include assessment worksheets, discussion questions for couples, and actionable strategies you can implement immediately. This isn't theoretical—it's applied wisdom.

5. Cultural Bridge

Having lived in Nigeria, Ghana, and South Africa, and having surveyed couples in both Africa and America, I bring perspective few relationship authors can offer. Whether you're navigating cross-cultural marriage or simply wanting to understand how culture shapes relationships, this book provides that bridge.

In many African traditions, a bridge is not merely a crossing but a communal threshold. One does not cross alone. Elders guide, witnesses observe, and the crossing carries responsibility to both where one has come from and where one is going. The second bridge in this book therefore represents not only personal transition, but a return to intentional relationship, collective accountability, and shared wisdom.

How to Use This Book

This book is organized into six parts, covering the complete relationship journey:

Part I: Foundations

The person you choose determines ninety percent of your happiness or misery — yet most people choose with their eyes closed. This Part introduces the Three Pillars — Trust, Appreciation, and Respect — and the eight compatibility factors that predict lasting love far more reliably than chemistry or passion.

Part II: The Journey

The hard conversations couples avoid before the wedding become the problems that end the marriage. Part Two argues that courtship is not romance — it is structured evaluation, and commitment without clarity is hope dressed as a plan.

Part III: Building and Sustaining

Relationships do not maintain themselves — they either grow or decay. This section addresses the five domains that determine whether a marriage thrives: money, faith, faithfulness, children, and daily connection.

Part IV: Family Dynamics

Part Four faces what most relationship books avoid; communication breakdown, counselling stigma, external pressures, polygamy, and single parenthood.

Part V: Challenges and Solutions

Marriage does not fail in isolation; it is shaped by external pressures, neglected communication, and delayed intervention. This section explores relationship influencers, the role of counselling, and why communication remains the foundation of everything. It argues that most challenges are survivable — if addressed early and honestly.

Part VI: Marriage Ends and Begins Again

Not every marriage reaches old age together. This part examines divorce, healing, and the possibility of second chances. It reframes endings not as the collapse of love, but as an opportunity for deeper self-awareness and wiser rebuilding.

Part VII: The Long View – Aging Together & Legacy

Marriage is not only about surviving conflict; it is about enduring across time. This section considers aging, companionship in later years, and the legacy couples leave behind. It asks not just how to stay together — but what kind of story your union will tell.

You can read this book cover to cover, or jump to the chapters most relevant to your current situation. Each chapter stands alone while contributing to a comprehensive understanding of relationships. Use the discussion questions with your partner to facilitate important conversations. Complete the assessment worksheets to gain clarity about your relationship. Take what resonates and apply it immediately.

This book is your companion whether you're planning to go into a new relationship, maintaining and growing an existing one, preparing for marriage, struggling in one, recovering from divorce, or building something new. The wisdom here is hard-won, research-backed, and proven in real life—both in what doesn't work and what finally does.

The Second Bridge Relationship Model

Foundation – Communication
Everything rests on communication. When communication breaks down, the entire bridge weakens.
Pillars – Trust, Appreciation, Respect
These are the structural supports of the relationship. If one pillar cracks, the bridge begins to tilt.
The Bridge – Partner Selection Factors
These determine whether the relationship is protected from future pressure. Choosing poorly here exposes the relationship to long-term strain.

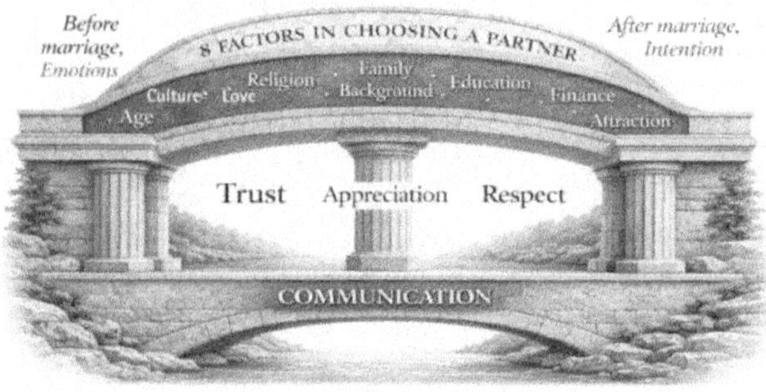

Figure 1

How to Use the Reflections and Assessments

At the end of each chapter, you will find a short section titled Reflection & Assessment. These prompts are designed to help you pause, think honestly, and—where applicable—engage your partner in meaningful conversation.

These reflections are not tests to pass or failures to fear. They are mirrors. Some you may answer easily; others may take time. Return to them as your relationship evolves.

You may choose to:

Reflect privately and journal your responses

Discuss the questions with your partner

Revisit the assessments periodically to notice growth or emerging gaps

The Couple Agreement Audit

The questions in this book are just the beginning. I've developed a comprehensive Agreement Audit—50 questions across 10 critical areas that reveal exactly where you're aligned and where you're not with your partner. At the end of this book is the first 3 of 10 Sections which I invite you to complete with your partner. To download your full free copy of The Couple Agreement Audit, scan the code after the questions.

My Promise to You

I promise you honesty over perfection. I promise you practical application over theoretical ideals. I promise you respect for your culture, your circumstances, and your journey—wherever you are right now.

I won't pretend relationships are easy. They're not. I won't pretend love conquers all. It doesn't. I won't pretend staying together is always right. Sometimes it isn't. But I will show you what I've learned from 35 years of struggle, 225 respondents surveyed across two continents, and a second marriage that's teaching me daily what healthy partnership looks like. I'll share the data on what really matters. I'll provide the tools to build or rebuild. I'll validate your experiences and offer hope that it's never too late to create something better. Whether you're 25 and just starting or 63 and starting again, the principles of healthy relationships remain the same. The question is: are you ready to learn them?

The journey begins now. Let's build that second bridge together.
Johannesburg, South Africa
January 2026

PART I - FOUNDATIONS: BEFORE THE COMMITMENT

Our cross-cultural survey of 225 respondents reveals that successful relationships rest on universal foundations, though cultural context shapes how these foundations are built. When selecting partners, respondents prioritize substance over surface. Education level leads the rankings (54-62% agreement), followed by religious compatibility (36-61%, with dramatic cultural variation), and family background (31-52%). Physical attributes—height, beauty, even race—rank at the bottom of both lists, with under 35% considering them important. This hierarchy suggests mature recognition that lasting relationships require intellectual and value compatibility, not just physical attraction.

The African data uniquely measures love's importance, and the results challenge Western assumptions about "traditional" cultures prioritizing pragmatic matches. A remarkable 77% of African respondents rate love as "very" or "extremely" important—higher than any other measured factor. Love, the data suggests, transcends cultural boundaries as the heart of relationship formation.

Pause for Reflection

This part of *The Second Bridge* is designed to be read as a whole. Before moving to the next section, you are invited to pause and reflect on the ideas explored across all the chapters in this part.

A short reflection questionnaire is available to help you assess insights, patterns, and areas for growth.

Please complete the questionnaire only after reading all chapters in this part. (Scan the code at the end of this section to access the reflection.)

CHAPTER 1: RELATIONSHIP FOUNDATIONS

*We don't inherit our capacity for relationships—we build it,
one experience at a time.*

The book's framework of - Trust, Appreciation, and Respect as foundational pillars - receives strong empirical support. Our survey reveals that trust levels correlate directly with relationship happiness: 89% of African respondents and 93% of USA respondents who trust their partners also report being happy in their relationships.

Our cross-cultural research confirms what wisdom traditions have long taught: trust forms the bedrock of lasting relationships. Among 225 respondents from two continents, those who trust their partners report happiness rates exceeding 85%, regardless of cultural background, income level, or religious affiliation.

The Question That Haunted Me

For years after my divorce, one question haunted me: How did I, a Leadership and Executive Coach who helps others navigate complex challenges—end up in a 35-year marriage that never really worked? The answer, I discovered, wasn't simple. It wasn't just about choosing the wrong person or making bad decisions. It went deeper—to the very foundations that shape our capacity for relationships long before we meet that first serious partner.

This chapter explores those foundations: the invisible architecture that determines not just who we choose, but how we love, communicate, and sustain partnerships. Understanding these foundations is the first step toward building relationships that last—or recognizing why past ones didn't (See Chapter 4 for research results).

The Five Pillars That Shape Us

Think of relationship capacity as a house. Long before you choose a partner, five foundational pillars are already in place, built from your earliest experiences:

1. Place of Birth and Environment

I was born in a polygamous household where my father had multiple wives. This wasn't unusual—it was our normal. Growing up in this environment taught me certain relationship patterns before I could even articulate them:

- Competition for attention and resources was built into family dynamics
- Fairness was constantly negotiated, never assumed
- Love could be divided among many without diminishing
- Authority was hierarchical—the patriarch decided, others adapted
- Emotional expression was often indirect, filtered through cultural protocol

Compare this to someone raised in urban America in the same era. Their foundational experiences might include nuclear family structures, emphasis on individual expression, romantic love as the primary relationship motivation, and egalitarian partnership models. Neither is right or wrong—but they're profoundly different starting points.

Your environment doesn't just shape what you believe about relationships—it shapes what you expect, what feels normal, what triggers discomfort, and what you unconsciously recreate or rebel against.

2. Family Upbringing and Lasting Impact

Beyond the general environment, your specific family taught you relationship templates through thousands of micro-interactions. These templates operate largely unconsciously, emerging when you're stressed, triggered, or navigating conflict. In my polygamous household, I learned:

- How to navigate complex family politics
- That women's power was often exercised indirectly
- That conflict was managed through intermediaries, not direct confrontation
- That personal needs often came after family obligations

When I entered my first marriage at 25, I unconsciously brought these patterns with me. My wife, raised in a different family structure, brought her own templates. Neither of us examined these assumptions explicitly. We just lived them out—and collided repeatedly.

Here's what I wish I'd understood then: Your family patterns aren't destiny, but they are your default programming. Without conscious examination and intentional change, you'll recreate what you know—even what you hated. When asked the question "What did you consider in choosing your partner?" in my survey, two of the five respondents said "Family background."

3. Culture, Tradition, and Relationship Expectations

Culture operates at a deeper level than we often recognize. It's not just about food preferences or holiday celebrations—it's about fundamental assumptions regarding:

• Who makes decisions and how
• What marriage is primarily for (companionship, procreation, economic partnership, family alliance)
• How conflict should be handled
• The role of extended family in the marriage
• How emotions should be expressed (or suppressed)
• What constitutes respect, honour, and appropriate behaviour

African family and relational systems were historically grounded in communal responsibility rather than individual fulfilment. As Ngũgĩ wa Thiong'o argues, colonial disruption reshaped African identity and social organisation, leaving modern African families negotiating between inherited communal values and imported individualist ideals (wa Thiong'o, 1986). This tension continues to shape expectations of marriage, authority, and emotional expression.

In traditional African culture, marriage joined families, not just individuals. Parents' approval is not just preferred—it is essential. The wedding isn't primarily about the couple's love story—it is about properly honouring both families and establishing the foundation for future generations.

When I married my first wife through family introduction, we were following cultural scripts of knowing each other's families, social standing, and character in the community. But it hadn't taught us about each other—not really. Cultural tradition valued these external factors over personal compatibility, emotional connection, or communication alignment.

The challenge for modern couples—especially cross-cultural ones—is recognizing that these deep cultural assumptions exist, surface them explicitly, and decide consciously which to honour and which to adapt.

4. Education's Role in Relationship Dynamics

Education shapes relationships in ways that extend far beyond earning potential. It influences:
- Communication styles and vocabulary
- Problem-solving approaches
- Worldview and openness to different perspectives
- Career expectations and life trajectory
- Social circles and cultural exposure
- Power dynamics within the relationship

When asked the question "What did you consider in choosing your partner?" in my survey, an Africa male's only response was "Intellect." My first wife and I had different education levels. This created subtle but persistent challenges in how we processed conflicts, made decisions, and envisioned our future. Neither of us was wrong—we simply thought differently, valued different things, and approached problem-solving from incompatible angles.

Education gaps don't doom relationships, but they require conscious bridge-building. Couples need to recognize the gap exists, value what each perspective brings, and develop shared languages for navigating differences.

My current marriage is between two people with similar education levels and professional experience. The difference is palpable. We speak the same language—literally and figuratively. Our problem-solving approaches align. Our career ambitions don't compete but complement. This compatibility creates ease where my first marriage had constant friction.

5. Premarital Life and Early Exposure

How you learned about relationships—from family dynamics, peer relationships, sex education, early dating experiences, or cultural messaging—shapes your relationship patterns in profound ways. I grew up in an environment where:
- Interactions with the opposite sex were carefully regulated
- Sex education was virtually non-existent
- Dating as courtship was not the cultural norm
- Attended a boarding boys-only high school
- Marriage readiness was assumed to come with age, not preparation

This meant I entered marriage without fundamental knowledge about emotional intimacy, sexual communication, conflict navigation with a romantic partner, or the daily reality of partnership. My wife had similar gaps. We were both learning on the job—with no instruction manual and no framework for discussing what we didn't know. This partly motivated me to write this book to equip the young and old people alike with the tools to navigate relationships.

Contrast this with my second marriage, where both of us had previous relationship experience, conscious preparation through counselling, and the maturity to discuss expectations openly. The foundation was entirely different—not because of age, but because of intentional preparation.

The Three Pillars of Healthy Relationships

Beyond these foundational shapers, three essential pillars support every healthy relationship. Without all three, the structure eventually weakens and collapses.

Trust: The Foundation of Everything

Trust emerges as the most consistent predictor of relationship satisfaction across both continents. The data shows remarkably similar trust levels:

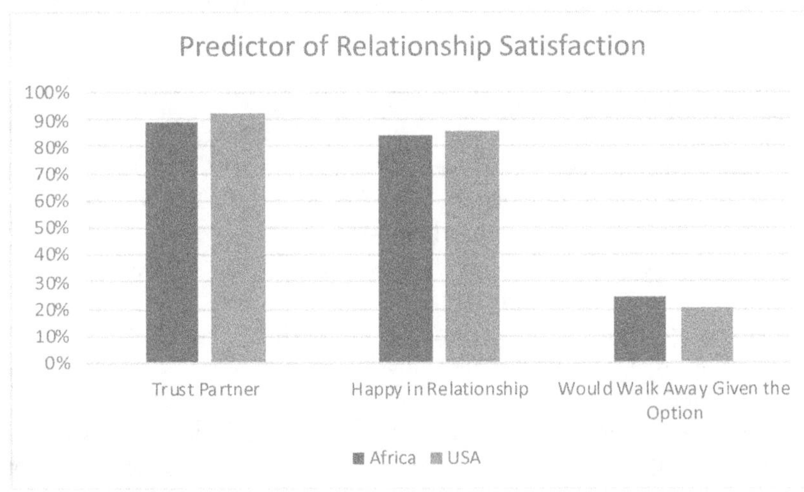

In my survey that asked specifically: Do you trust your spouse and why? A married African male said:

Yes, I do because over time, different situations have manifested and these have given me a chance to know her deeply and this has led to the development of trust

All the 5 respondents interviewed said yes when they were asked if they trusted their spouses.

The correlation between trust and happiness is consistent across cultures, suggesting trust is a universal relationship requirement rather than a cultural preference. Trust isn't just about fidelity or keeping promises—though those matters. It's about:

• Emotional safety: Can you be vulnerable without fear of mockery or weaponization?

• Reliability: Does your partner follow through on commitments?

• Integrity: Do their actions match their words?

• Transparency: Can you discuss difficult topics honestly?

• Consistency: Is their behaviour predictable enough to feel secure?

In my first marriage, trust eroded gradually through thousands of small disappointments, unmet expectations, and unspoken resentments. We never had a major betrayal—just a slow leak that eventually emptied the reservoir completely.

My second marriage demonstrated what trust looks like when built intentionally from the start. We established patterns of honest communication immediately. We address issues when they're small. We follow through on commitments. We don't weaponize vulnerabilities shared in confidence. This creates a foundation where both partners feel safe to be fully themselves.

Appreciation: The Oxygen of Partnership

Appreciation isn't just saying 'thank you'—though that helps. It's genuinely valuing what your partner brings to the relationship, even when it's different from what you would bring. In my first marriage, we stopped appreciating each other years before we stopped functioning as partners. We saw each other's contributions as obligatory, not valuable. We noticed deficits, not strengths. We criticized freely but praised rarely. This created a toxic cycle: less appreciation led to less effort, which led to more criticism, which led to defensiveness and withdrawal. Eventually, we were two people coexisting rather than partnering.

My current relationship taught me what consistent appreciation creates: motivation to keep contributing, willingness to be vulnerable, pride in the partnership, resilience during difficult seasons, and joy in daily life together. We make appreciation explicit. Not performative, not manipulative, but genuine recognition of effort, sacrifice, thoughtfulness, and love. This simple practice transforms the emotional climate of a relationship.

Respect: The Guardian of Dignity

Respect is treating your partner's needs, opinions, and dignity as equally important to your own—even when you disagree, especially when you're angry. Respect manifests in:

- How you speak to each other, particularly during conflict
- How you speak about each other to others
- Whether you protect each other's dignity publicly
- How you handle differences of opinion
- Whether you honour boundaries and preferences
- How you respond to mistakes and failures

One of the most painful aspects of my first marriage was the gradual erosion of respect. We said things in anger we couldn't take back. We dismissed each other's concerns. We made unilateral decisions that affected both of us. We stopped protecting each other's dignity.

In my second marriage, we established a non-negotiable rule: we never disrespect each other, even in private, even when frustrated. We don't call each other names. We don't mock. We don't dismiss. We disagree—often—but we do it respectfully. This single commitment has prevented countless small wounds that accumulate into permanent damage.

Moving Forward: From Foundation to Future

Your relationship foundations—your environment, family upbringing, culture, education, and early exposure—shaped your starting point. But they don't determine your destination.

I grew up in a polygamous household with minimal relationship education, married through family introduction without truly knowing my partner, and struggled for 35 years with patterns I never examined. Those foundations predicted my first marriage outcome. But at 61, I examined those foundations consciously. I identified what didn't work and why. I clarified what I needed. I built intentional patterns with my second wife from day one. Those same foundations—now examined and addressed—contributed to an entirely different outcome.

The foundations matter. Understanding them matters more. But conscious choice—examining your patterns, intentionally building the three pillars, and communicating openly—matters most of all. You can't change where you started. But you can absolutely change where you're going. That's the promise of relationship foundations: not determinism, but awareness. Not limitation, but possibility. Not fate, but choice. And that choice—to examine, understand, and intentionally build on your foundations—is where lasting relationships begin.

Reflection & Assessment

Personal Reflection

What relationship patterns did I witness growing up, and how have they shaped me?

Which behaviours from my family of origin do I consciously repeat?

Do I believe relationships succeed by effort, fate, or sacrifice?

Partner Dialogue

What did love look like in your home growing up?

Which relationship patterns do you want to continue—and which do you want to break?

Reality Check Rate each statement from 1 (Strongly Disagree) to 5 (Strongly Agree):

I understand how my upbringing influences my relationships

I take responsibility for my emotional patterns

KEY TAKEAWAYS

• Five foundational factors shape your relationship capacity: place of birth/environment, family upbringing, culture/tradition, education, and early exposure

• Three essential pillars support every healthy relationship: trust, appreciation, and respect—without all three, the structure collapses

• Communication is the bridge that connects two individuals into a functioning partnership

• Similar backgrounds ease initial adjustment but don't guarantee success; different backgrounds can strengthen relationships if navigated consciously

• Unexamined foundations create unconscious conflict; conscious examination leads to healthy partnerships

• Your foundations don't determine your destiny—conscious choice does

CHAPTER 2: IN THE BEGINNING—CHOOSING WISELY

The person you choose to marry will determine 90% of your happiness or misery.

When choosing partners, our respondents reveal a clear hierarchy that may surprise some readers:

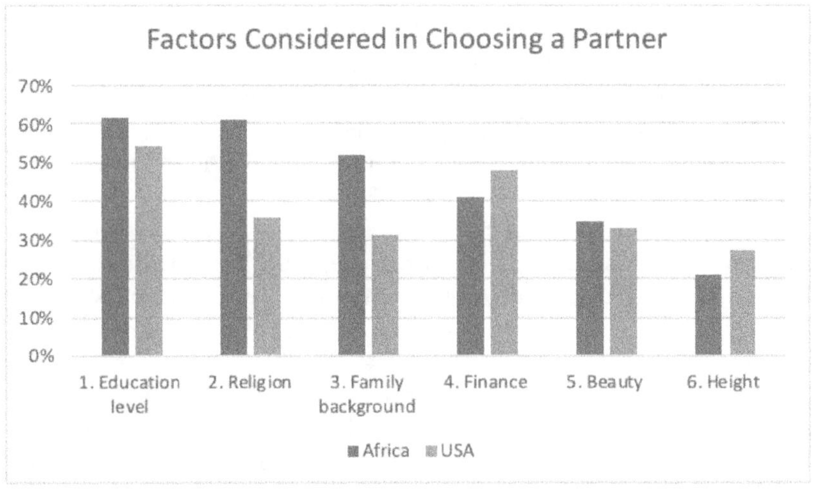

Contrary to romantic movie narratives, physical attraction ranks among the lowest priorities for partner selection across both continents. Our research shows that practical factors—education, values, family background—consistently outrank appearance. This doesn't diminish attraction's role; rather, it places it in proper perspective within the broader picture of lasting compatibility.

The Choice I Made at 25

I made the most important decision of my life with almost no information. This wasn't unusual in traditional Nigerian culture. In the past, there have been stories of people who got married on the basis of seeing the bride's or groom's photograph only. In fact, it was the norm. The assumption was that family compatibility, cultural alignment, and proper upbringing were more important than personal chemistry or emotional connection. If the families approved and the social credentials checked out, the marriage would work. Love would grow. Partnership would develop.

I can tell you: those assumptions were catastrophically wrong. But here's what I learned: the problem wasn't the choice I made. I followed a scrip, and my absolute belief that things would work out for good and that I will make it work. I never asked the fundamental question: Do I actually know this person well enough to build a life with her?

Culture Shock as Wake-Up Call

Years into my first marriage, I had an experience that crystallized everything. I worked in Nigeria, Ghana and South Africa and visited over 40 countries across the world. The cultural difference was profound—not just in language or customs, but in fundamental assumptions about relationships, communication, individuality, and partnership.

I watched couples interact with an ease and directness that felt foreign. They disagreed openly but respectfully. They made decisions together through discussion, not assumption. They expressed affection casually. They seemed to genuinely enjoy each other's company—not just coexist.

The culture shock wasn't about the countries I lived in and visited. It was about realizing that the patterns I had accepted as inevitable— the distance, the unspoken tensions, the parallel lives—weren't inevitable at all. Other ways of relating were possible. I just hadn't known to look for them when choosing a partner. My travels around the world planted a seed: What if I had chosen differently? What if I had known what questions to ask, what compatibility really meant, what actually matters for building a life together?

The Second Time: Choosing with Eyes Wide Open

Fast forward to my second marriage, everything was different as I was equipped with the Foundation of relationships (Chapter 1). This time, I had:

• Thirty-five years of experience of what doesn't work

- Research from 225 respondents revealing what does work
- Clarity about my values, needs, and non-negotiables
- The maturity to ask hard questions and hear honest answers
- The willingness to walk away if the fit wasn't right

When a friend introduced me to the woman who would become my current wife, I approached it entirely differently. We didn't just enjoy each other's company—we interrogated our compatibility. We didn't assume love would conquer all—we examined whether our life visions aligned. In fact, she did a background check on me by asking for references some of whom were my family members. I did the same thing.

We didn't rush into commitment—we did marriage coaching before the wedding to address potential challenges proactively. Four months after meeting, we married. Not because we were swept away by emotion, but because we had methodically verified compatibility across every dimension that matters: values, communication styles, financial approaches, life goals, conflict resolution patterns, expectations about marriage, and willingness to work as a team.

The difference between my two marriages started with the difference in how I chose. The first time, I followed tradition and self-belief. The second time, I made conscious decision and chose wisely.

Environmental and Cultural Compatibility

One of the most underestimated factors in partner selection is environmental and cultural compatibility. We often focus on personality traits or shared interests, overlooking the deeper patterns shaped by where and how someone grew up.

The Weight of Environment

Your partner's environment shaped them in ways they may not even recognize:

- Climate and lifestyle: Someone raised in tropical Lagos has different daily rhythms and expectations than someone from temperate London
- Urban versus rural: City dwellers often value independence and privacy; rural communities often prioritize collective decision-making and family involvement
- Economic context: Growing up wealthy versus poor shapes attitudes about money, security, and what constitutes 'enough'
- Family stability: Someone who grew up in a stable family has different risk tolerance than someone who experienced upheaval

My ex-wife and I came from similar backgrounds, which masked deeper differences. I grew up in a polygamous household with complex family politics; she was brought up by a single mother. These environmental differences created friction we didn't anticipate because we hadn't examined them explicitly.

The Culture Question

Culture isn't just ethnicity or nationality. It's the invisible water you swim in—the assumptions you don't even know you're making:

• How do you define family? (Nuclear versus extended, blood versus chosen)

• What's the role of elders? (Respected advisors versus authority figures)

• How do you handle conflict? (Direct confrontation versus indirect communication versus avoidance)

• What's the purpose of marriage? (Love and companionship versus procreation versus economic security)

• How do you view gender roles? (Egalitarian versus traditional versus negotiable)

In my second marriage, my wife and I share similar professional backgrounds, faith, have both lived in stable families, and are equipped with the necessary tools to cross The Bridge. Though from different cultural background, these created solid foundation for negotiating our differences. We don't assume our way is the only way.

The Practical Realities: Food, Climate, and Lifestyle

This sounds trivial until you're living it. The daily friction of incompatible practical preferences wears down even strong relationships.

Food and Dietary Compatibility

You eat two meals a day and your partner eats three meals a day. One partner is vegetarian and the other carnivorous, one loves spicy food and the other can't tolerate it, one has religious dietary restrictions and the other doesn't—these aren't minor inconveniences. They're daily negotiations.

In my first marriage, we came from similar food cultures, which was one area of ease. In my second marriage, we both enjoy diverse cuisines and are willing to compromise.

Climate and Geographic Preferences

Can someone who thrives in cold climates be happy in tropical heat? Can someone who lives in the mountains tolerate flat plains? Can a city person adapt to rural life?

I've lived in Nigeria, Ghana, and South Africa—all warm climates. My comfort zone is established. If I had fallen in love with someone whose dream was to live in Scandinavia, we would have had a fundamental incompatibility that no amount of love could overcome. One of us would have been perpetually uncomfortable.

Lifestyle and Daily Rhythms

Are you a morning person or night owl? Do you need quiet or thrive on activity? Do you prefer spontaneity or planning? Do you need alone time or constant connection?

My current wife goes to bed at a specific time, whilst I stay up late; we value structured time, but also appreciate spontaneity. We both need some alone time daily, but also prioritize connection and pray together. These alignments weren't luck—we verified them during courtship.

Making Conscious Choices About Partner Background

The point isn't that you need identical backgrounds, which is a challenge in today's world. It's that you need conscious awareness of how your backgrounds differ and a shared commitment to bridging those differences.

Questions to Ask Before Committing

Here are the questions I wish I had asked:

1. About Environment and Upbringing:

• Where do you feel most at home? Why?

• What aspects of your childhood environment do you want to recreate? What do you want to avoid?

• How did your family handle conflict? Money? Decision-making?

• What did you learn about marriage from your parents' relationship?

2. About Culture and Values:

• What cultural traditions are non-negotiable for you? Which are you willing to adapt?

• What role will our extended families play in our marriage?

• How do you define success in life? In marriage?

• What are your core values? (Name your top five)

3. About Practical Compatibility:

• Where do you envision living long-term? Is that negotiable?

• What does your ideal daily life look like?

- How important is it that we share meals? Hobbies? Friends?
- What are your deal-breakers in a living situation?

When Opposites Attract: Can It Work?

The old saying 'opposites attract' contains truth—but it's incomplete. Opposites do attract initially. The question is: can they build and hold a sustainable partnership?

The Attraction Phase

Differences often create initial attraction because they're exciting:

- The introvert admires the extrovert's social ease
- The planner appreciates the spontaneous person's flexibility
- The cautious person enjoys the risk-taker's adventures but what attracts initially often irritates eventually:
- That social ease becomes 'never wants to stay home'
- That flexibility becomes 'unreliable and chaotic'
- Those adventures become 'reckless and financially irresponsible'

Making Opposites Work

Opposite personality types can build strong marriages—but only with:

Shared core values: You can differ in style but must align on what matters most

Mutual appreciation: Each partner values what the other brings rather than trying to change them

Clear communication: You explicitly discuss how your differences will be navigated

Willingness to compromise: Both partners adjust, not just one

Similar life goals: You want the same future, even if you'd get there differently

Sex Education and Relationship Readiness

One of the most underdiscussed factors in partner selection is whether both people are actually ready for the emotional and physical intimacy marriage requires.

What I Didn't Know at 25

I entered my first marriage with virtually no sex education conversation with my ex-wife. My ex-wife had similar gaps. We were both from conservative backgrounds where these topics simply weren't discussed. The result:

• We had no framework for discussing sexual expectations or preferences

• We didn't understand that sexual compatibility matters and can be discussed

• We had no tools for navigating differences or challenges

• We assumed issues would resolve themselves (they didn't)

The silence around intimacy wasn't just about sex—it reflected our broader inability to discuss difficult topics. If you can't talk about physical intimacy, you probably can't talk about emotional intimacy, financial stress, or parenting disagreements either.

Contemporary African voices continue to challenge silence around intimacy. Nana Darkoa Sekiyiamah's work highlights how unspoken emotional and sexual expectations often undermine connection, particularly when cultural restraint prevents honest dialogue (Sekyiamah, 2022).

What Relationship Readiness Actually Means

Before choosing a partner, ask yourself if you're ready for partnership:

• Can you discuss difficult topics without shutting down or exploding?

• Do you understand your own emotional patterns and triggers?

• Can you identify and communicate your needs?

• Are you capable of emotional vulnerability?

• Have you done work to understand how your upbringing affects your relationships?

I wasn't ready at 25. I had no self-awareness, no communication skills, no understanding of partnership. I chose to marry before I was equipped to be married. That's not unusual—many people do. But it dramatically increases the difficulty of building a healthy relationship.

Practical Application: Choosing Wisely Today

Whether you're choosing a first partner or a second one, the Three Pillars are important (See Chapter 1). In addition, here's how to do it wisely:

For Singles: Before You Choose

Do your own work first: Understand yourself before trying to understand a partner

Get clear on non-negotiables: What do you absolutely need? What can you definitely not tolerate?

Look beyond chemistry: Attraction matters, but compatibility matters more

Have the hard conversations early: Don't wait until after commitment to discuss deal-breakers

Observe how they handle stress: Anyone can be pleasant when things are easy

Meet their family: You're not just marrying them; you're joining their family system

Trust your gut: If something feels off, investigate it rather than ignoring it

For Those Already Committed: Deepening Understanding

If you're already married or committed, you can still apply these principles:

Have the conversations you skipped: It's never too late to discuss foundational topics

Name the differences explicitly: Stop pretending incompatibilities don't exist

Develop bridge-building skills: Learn to navigate differences consciously

Seek pre-emptive help: Don't wait for crisis to get counselling

Moving Forward: The Courage to Choose Consciously

Choosing wisely requires courage. It means asking hard questions that might reveal incompatibilities. It means being willing to walk away from someone you're attracted to if the fundamentals don't align. It means disappointing family or cultural expectations. It means doing the uncomfortable work of self-examination.

At 25, I lacked that courage. I followed the path of least resistance. I trusted tradition over investigation. I chose comfort over clarity. I thought I could make it work despite our obvious differences.

At 61, I had developed that courage. I asked every hard question. I verified every important compatibility. I walked through discomfort to reach clarity. I chose with eyes wide open.

The contrast in those two choices shaped the difference in those two marriages.

Your choice of partner is the single most important decision you'll make. Choose wisely. Choose consciously. Choose with courage. Your future happiness depends on it.

Reflection & Assessment

Personal Reflection
What need was I trying to meet when I chose my partner?
Did I choose from clarity or urgency?
What warning signs did I ignore—and why?
Partner Dialogue
Why do you think we chose each other?
What do you believe truly holds us together today?
Reality Check Tick all that apply:
☐ My choice was values-based

☐ My choice was pressure-based

☐ My choice was fear-based

☐ My choice was intentional

KEY TAKEAWAYS

• The person you choose determines 90% of your happiness or misery—choose with eyes wide open

• Environmental and cultural compatibility matter deeply—discuss differences explicitly before committing

• Practical realities (food, climate, lifestyle) create daily friction if incompatible—don't dismiss them as trivial

• Opposites can attract and build lasting partnerships—but only with shared values, mutual appreciation, and explicit agreements

• Relationship readiness matters as much as partner choice—do your own work first

• Have hard conversations early—don't wait until after commitment to discuss deal-breakers

CHAPTER 3: REASONS PEOPLE ENTER RELATIONSHIPS

Respect is the oxygen of love; once it thins, the relationship begins to suffocate.

Why do people enter relationships? It seems like a simple question, but the answers are as varied as the people themselves. In my research across two continents, I discovered that while everyone claims love is the reason, the truth is often more complex. Understanding the real motivations—both yours and your partner's, in addition to the Three Pillars (See Chapter 1), can mean the difference between a relationship that thrives and one that struggles.

Love Remains Supreme

The African survey data provides powerful evidence that love, not convenience or obligation, drives relationship formation. A remarkable 77.4% of African respondents rate love as "very" or "extremely" important in their relationship considerations.

Those who assume African relationships are primarily practical arrangements driven by family or financial considerations misunderstand the cultural reality. Our survey of 87 African respondents from Kenya, Nigeria, Uganda, South Africa, and Ghana reveals that love remains the paramount consideration—over three-quarters rate it as very or extremely important. This challenges Western stereotypes while affirming the universal human desire for genuine emotional connection.

The Seven Primary Motivations

Through my research and personal observations, I've identified seven primary reasons people enter relationships. Most people have a combination of these motivations, but usually one stands out as the driving force.

1. Love - The Essential Foundation

This is what everyone claims first. "I'm in love," we say, and it feels like the most natural thing in the world. But what is love, really?

Sobonfu Somé describes love in African cosmology not as a private emotion but as a communal and spiritual practice, sustained through responsibility, honesty, and collective accountability (Somé, 1999). In my Nigerian childhood, I watched my father navigate relationships with multiple wives. What I observed taught me that love manifests differently across cultures and even within the same household. The romantic love celebrated in American movies looked nothing like the pragmatic partnership I saw in many African marriages, yet both could be genuine.

True love—the kind that sustains a marriage through decades—is more than the butterflies you feel when you first meet someone. It's a choice you make every day to prioritize your partner's wellbeing alongside your own. It's patient when frustrated, kind when tired, and faithful when tempted.

2. Children - The Procreation Factor

In many African cultures, marriage and children are practically synonymous. The question isn't whether you'll have children, but how many and how soon. One common greeting after "How are you?" is "How is your family?" which represents you, your spouse and children. Once you are married, the next question is when are you having children? This question is often asked by friends, parents, in-laws and every other person who believes they have a stake in your well-being.

This perspective might shock those outside of Africa, but it's deeply rooted in cultures where children represent security, legacy, and the continuation of family lines. Some cultures not only emphasise children, they openly show preference for a male child. In societies without robust retirement systems, children are literally your future caregivers.

However, entering a relationship primarily for procreation creates specific challenges. What happens when:

- Children don't come as expected?
- One partner changes their mind about wanting children?
- The children grow up and leave home?

There are marriages where children were the glue holding everything together—and when those children left for college, the parents looked at each other and realized they had nothing else in common. They had been co-parents, not partners.

Conversely, there are others who deeply wanted children, but are faced with infertility, while some chose not to have children. Those who had built their relationship on a foundation broader than procreation survived and even thrived. Those who hadn't often struggled or separated.

3. Wealth - Financial Security and Influence

We're often told that marrying for money is somehow morally wrong. The truth is more nuanced. There's a difference between seeking financial security and seeking to exploit someone's wealth. A woman who wants a partner who is financially responsible and can contribute to building a stable household is being practical. A woman who targets rich men for their money while offering nothing in return is being predatory. The distinction matters.

In some cultures in Africa, financial considerations are openly discussed during marriage arrangements. "What is his earning potential? What assets does her family bring?" These are not considered crude questions but responsible ones. The goal wasn't exploitation but ensuring the couple had a foundation for building their life together. When asked the question "What role does money play in your relationship currently?" four of the five African respondents said money is important with one saying "Money is an enabler" and another saying "Money plays a vital role."

In some other cultures, people are embarrassed to discuss money before marriage, as if bringing up finances somehow tainted the purity of love. Yet these same couples often fought bitterly about money within the first year of marriage because they had never aligned their financial values and expectations. The key is being honest about your motivations and ensuring your partner understands and agrees.

4. Power - Association with Influential People

Some people enter relationships to gain access to power, status, or influential networks. This motivation is more common than people admit, particularly in certain professional circles. In some cases, strategic marriages and family connections can advance careers and create powerful alliances. Even in faiths, some people pursue relationships with the spiritual leader's children or spiritual leaders to gain spiritual status or influence.

Is this wrong? Not necessarily. Problems arise when:
 • One party is aware of the power motivation and the other isn't

• The relationship is entirely transactional with no genuine affection

• The less powerful partner is being used and discarded once they're no longer needed

However, seeking a partner who shares your ambitions and can help you achieve your goals isn't inherently problematic. My wife and support each other's careers and dreams. We open doors for each other and leveraged our combined network. This isn't manipulation—it's partnership. The question to ask yourself: If your partner lost their status, position, or connections tomorrow, would you still want to be with them? If the answer is yes, you're in a partnership. If the answer is no or you're unsure, you might be pursuing power rather than love.

5. Security - Faithfulness and Protection

Particularly among women, though not exclusively, the desire for security drives many relationship decisions. This encompasses emotional security, physical safety, and the assurance of faithfulness.

Security as a primary motivation isn't shallow—it's human. We all want to feel safe, protected, and confident that our partner won't abandon or betray us. Problems arise when security becomes the only factor, overriding all other considerations, including compatibility, respect, and mutual growth.

I've watched women and some men stay in unfulfilling or even harmful relationships because they fear the insecurity of being alone. Security without love, respect, and genuine partnership isn't security at all—it's a prison.

6. Religion - Spiritual Alignment

For many people, particularly those with strong faith convictions, shared religious beliefs are non-negotiable (See more on Religion in Chapter 10). In most religions, faith is the centre of life. Some people wouldn't marry someone who didn't share their faith, as it affects how decisions are made in the family, how children are raised, and how to find meaning in the event of a crisis.

Religious motivation for marriage can create incredibly strong bonds when both partners are equally committed. I've known couples where shared faith was the foundation of a beautiful partnership. I've also seen relationships where religion became a weapon, with one partner using religion to control or manipulate the other.

The key question: Is your faith drawing you together and helping you become better partners, or is it creating division and control?

7. Societal Expectations - Cultural Pressure

Perhaps the least discussed but most powerful motivation is societal pressure. In many cultures—African, Asian, Middle Eastern, and even some American subcultures—remaining unmarried past a certain age brings shame, questions, and social marginalization.

In most African cultures, when a woman is over 28 years of age, on average, people would start asking, "When will you get marry? What's wrong with you?" Your younger sister is already married with children. The pressure from family could be unbearable. Some women above that age accept marriage proposals because they are unable to stand the shame anymore.

The pressure comes from multiple sources:
• Parents worried about who will care for their aging daughter/son
• The extended family concerned about their reputation
• Religious communities that emphasize marriage as God's plan
• Cultural norms that define adulthood by marital status
• Friends whose marriages make you feel left behind

In America, where individualism is celebrated, the pressure exists. Women approaching or past 30 often feel panic. Men are questioned about their masculinity or sexuality if they remain unmarried. And for both genders, attending yet another wedding alone while fielding questions about when it will be "your turn" creates intense pressure to settle.

Marriages entered primarily due to societal pressure face significant challenges. Without genuine love and compatibility as foundations, these relationships often become situations to endure rather than partnerships to celebrate.

Understanding Your Primary Motivation

Here's an exercise I recommend for anyone considering marriage or evaluating their current relationship:

List the seven motivations in order of their importance to you:

1. ____
2. ____
3. ____
4. ____
5. ____
6. ____
7. ____

Now, honestly answer: What was my primary motivation for entering (or considering) this relationship?

Then, ask your partner to do the same exercise and compare answers. You might be surprised by what you discover.

When Multiple Motivations Coexist

Most healthy relationships involve multiple motivations. I married my ex-wife because I loved her (motivation #1), but also because we shared faith (motivation #6), wanted to build a family (motivation #2), and yes, because at a certain point, I was ready for marriage and she represented everything I thought I was looking for (motivation #7— though I didn't realize societal expectations played a role until years later).

The question isn't whether you have multiple motivations—most people do, rather, the relevant questions should be:

• Are you honest with yourself about them?

• Does your partner understand and share them?

• Are any of your motivations fundamentally incompatible with a healthy partnership?

• What happens if your primary motivation changes or becomes impossible?

When Motivations Shift

Here's what many relationship books don't tell you: motivations evolve. The love that brought you together might deepen into something more profound—or it might fade. The desire for children might be fulfilled, leaving you wondering what comes next. Financial security might improve or deteriorate. Religious devotion might strengthen or weaken.

The couples who thrive are those who:

1. Recognize when motivations shift
2. Communicate honestly about the changes
3. Actively work to build new shared motivations
4. Don't cling to outdated reasons for staying together

I've seen couples who married primarily for children become deeply connected partners after the kids left home—because they intentionally nurtured their relationship beyond parenting. I've also seen couples divorce the day their youngest graduated high school because they had built nothing else.

Practical Guidance

Before committing to a relationship, have honest conversations about motivations:

"What drew you to me initially?"

"What are you hoping marriage will provide for you?"

"How important is [love/children/financial security/faith/etc.] to you?"

"If [specific circumstance] changed, how would that affect your commitment?"

These conversations aren't romantic, but they're essential. Romance won't sustain you through infertility, job loss, health crises, or faith transitions. Knowing why you're together—truly knowing—will.

Red Flags

Watch for these warning signs:

• Reluctance to discuss motivations honestly

• Discovering your partner's primary motivation is something you cannot or will not provide

• Feeling pressure to become someone different to fulfil your partner's expectations

• Realizing you entered the relationship for reasons that no longer exist or never materialized

Reflection & Assessment

Personal Reflection

Was companionship, security, love, status, or expectation my primary motivation?

Do those reasons still exist in my current relationship?

Partner Dialogue

What did you hope this relationship would give you?

What has changed since then?

Reality Check Rate from 1–5:

My original reasons for entering this relationship still align with our current reality

The Deeper Truth About Motivation

There is no single "right" reason to enter a relationship. Love is powerful, but love alone does not sustain a marriage. Security matters. Faith matters. Children, finances, cultural expectations, and timing all matter—whether we admit it or not.

What ultimately determines the health of a relationship is not *which* motivations brought you together, but **how honestly you**

understand them and how openly you share them with your partner.

Problems begin when:

We deny our true motivations

We disguise fear as love

We expect our partner to fulfil needs they never agreed to carry

Or we cling to reasons for staying together that no longer exist

The strongest couples are not those with the "purest" motivations, but those with the **clearest self-awareness.** They know why they chose each other. They revisit that question as life changes. And when motivations shift—as they inevitably do—they talk about it rather than pretending nothing has changed.

Before moving forward, sit with this question longer than feels necessary: **Why am I really here?**

Not the version you tell friends. Not the version that sounds noble or romantic. **The real reason.**

Because once you understand why you seek partnership, you are finally ready to answer the next—and arguably more consequential—question: Who should I choose?

CHAPTER 4: FACTORS TO CONSIDER IN CHOOSING A PARTNER

Chemistry attracts, but compatibility sustains.

If motivation explains **why** we enter relationships, selection determines **whether those relationships survive**. Many people enter relationships for the right reasons—and still choose the wrong partner. Others choose partners who look perfect on paper, only to discover years later that they are deeply incompatible where it matters most.

Love may bring you together. Compatibility is what keeps you together.

In this chapter, we shift from internal drivers to external realities—from intention to execution. Drawing on survey data from 225 respondents across Africa and the United States, as well as years of lived experience, we explore the **practical factors that shape long-term relationship success.**

What people wish they had considered before marriage is often very different from what they actually did consider. This chapter is designed to close that gap.

The factors explored here are not about perfection. They are about **alignment**—in values, expectations, life direction, and daily living. Some differences enrich a marriage. Others quietly erode it.

Understanding these factors does not guarantee a perfect relationship. But ignoring them almost guarantees unnecessary struggle.

As you read, resist the urge to evaluate your partner alone. Evaluate yourself just as honestly. The goal is not to judge—but to choose wisely.

Because choosing a partner is not just a romantic decision. It is **a life-shaping decision**.

The Eight Critical Factors

Let me walk you through the eight factors that consistently emerged as most significant, along with how Americans and Africans ranked them differently—and what we can learn from those differences.

1. Love and Emotional Connection

As we saw in Chapter 3, love is a central motivation across cultures. Here, we shift from motive to match: how love translates into compatibility.

Ask yourself:

- Do I genuinely enjoy this person's company?
- Do I respect how they handle challenges?
- Do I admire their character, not just their accomplishments?
- Can I be fully myself around them?
- Do they bring out better or worse in me?

2. Education Level and Intellectual Compatibility

Education level emerges as the most universally valued partner selection criterion. This preference may reflect shared values, communication ability, economic potential, or intellectual compatibility. Survey results from partners across Africa and the USA revealed a strong consensus on the importance of education and intellectual compatibility in romantic relationships, with 62% of African respondents and 54% of American respondents prioritizing this factor. This notable alignment, despite cultural and geographic differences, underscores a universal desire for mental synergy that fosters deeper emotional bonds, meaningful conversations, and shared growth trajectories.

However, education level doesn't automatically equal intellectual compatibility. A PhD holder could marry someone with high school diplomas and still have stimulating conversations and shared curiosity about the world. Conversely, couples with identical degrees could bore each other to tears. The key isn't matching credentials but matching:

- Intellectual curiosity
- Ability to engage in meaningful conversation
- Respect for learning and growth
- Similar or complementary ways of processing information

Consider not just current education but attitudes toward learning, growth, and intellectual development. Will you grow together or apart?

3. Financial Stability and Expectations

Finance plays a nuanced role that differs between continents. While 48% of USA respondents consider finance important in partner selection (vs 41% Africa), African respondents more often cite it as playing a "very" or "extremely" important role in their actual relationships (38% vs 27%). Yet most couples don't discuss finances thoroughly before marriage.

This disconnect creates enormous problems. Most tellingly, among USA respondents who would leave their relationships if they could, 21% cite financial security as what prevents them—compared to only 2% in Africa.

Our research reveals a paradox: Americans are more likely to consider finance when choosing partners, yet Africans report money playing a larger role in their daily relationships. Perhaps most revealing, financial security keeps 21% of dissatisfied American couples together, compared to just 2% in Africa. This suggests American couples may be more financially interdependent—or more trapped by financial obligations—while African couples find other reasons to stay. Financial compatibility involves:
- Spending vs. saving orientation
- Views on debt
- Career ambitions and earning expectations
- How money will be managed (joint accounts, separate, hybrid)
- Financial obligations to extended family
- Standards of living expectations
- Retirement and long-term planning

Financial discussions to have before commitment:
- Current debt and financial obligations
- Spending habits and financial values
- Career plans and earning expectations
- Extended family financial responsibilities
- How you'll make financial decisions together
- Financial goals for 5, 10, 20 years
- How you'll handle financial setbacks

Couples who discussed money thoroughly before marriage rarely listed finances as their biggest challenge afterward. Those who avoided the conversation almost always regretted it.

4. Race and Cultural Background

Cross-cultural and interracial marriages are becoming more common, particularly in American urban areas and among educated Africans who've studied abroad. My current marriage bridges Nigerian and different South African cultural traditions and taught me that cultural compatibility requires more than good intentions.

Many participants felt bound not by their emotions, but by cultural and religious expectations that define what 'endurance' should look like in marriage. These obligations kept couples together, but often at the cost of unaddressed emotional needs.

For many African men and women, endurance in marriage has long been framed as moral strength rather than emotional suppression. What is often missing from this framing is permission—permission to speak, to question, and to acknowledge pain without being seen as disloyal to culture or family.

Cross-cultural relationships face unique challenges:
* Different communication styles (direct vs. indirect)
* Different family structures and obligations
* Different expectations about gender roles
* Different approaches to conflict resolution
* Different relationships with time and punctuality
* Different food preferences and lifestyle habits
* Different ways of raising children

These differences can enrich a marriage when approached with curiosity and respect. They can destroy it when approached with rigidity and judgment. Before committing to a cross-cultural relationship, honestly assess:
* How flexible are you, really?
* How will you handle family disapproval?
* Where will you live, and whose culture will dominate?
* How will you raise children with two cultural identities?
* Are you attracted to your partner or to their exotic "otherness"?
* Can you handle being a perpetual outsider in your partner's cultural community?

5. Age Difference Considerations

Cultural norms around age differences vary dramatically. In many African cultures, men marrying women 10-15 years younger is common and is expected.

In American progressive circles, even 5 years raises eyebrows if the man is older. Survey data showed:
* 47.6% of African respondents would consider age in making marriage decision
* And 35.6% of American respondents felt the same way
* But attitudes varied dramatically based on gender, religion, and region.

Age differences create specific dynamics:
• Power imbalances (especially when one partner is significantly more established)
  • Different life stages and energy levels
  • Different generational cultural references
  • Different timeline for children and family planning
  • Different health trajectories as you age
  • Potential for outliving your partner by decades
Age itself isn't destiny. What matters is:
  • Maturity levels (which don't always correlate with age)
  • Life stage alignment
  • Shared values and goals
  • Power balance in the relationship
  • How the age difference affects family and social acceptance

6. Social Status and Family Background

"When you marry someone, you marry their family." This isn't just a saying in African culture—it is absolute truth. And despite American emphasis on individualism, it remains true in the USA as well.

Survey responses revealed:
• 52.4% of African respondents rated family background as "very important"
• 30.9% of American respondents said the same

In my survey that asked: What role does family relations play in your marriage? A married African male said:

"Family is crucial in reaffirming that I am not only married to my spouse but into the family."

Another married African female said:

"Family relations play a vital role. Very core. All our family members (including in-laws on either side) are close and relate freely. The few that do not simply choose to of their own accord but would be free to relate whenever they opted.　　"

All the five respondents interviewed said family relations played an important role in their relationship.

Social status and family background matter because they shape:
  • Expectations about lifestyle
  • Communication patterns and conflict styles
  • Values around money, education, and success
  • Support systems (or lack thereof)
  • Obligations to extended family
  • Social networks and friendships
Questions to consider:

• How does your partner's family treat you?

• How does your family treat your partner?

• Are there significant class, education, or cultural differences between families?

• How will you handle family obligations and expectations?

• What happens if families never fully accept the marriage?

7. Physical Attraction and Chemistry

Let's be honest: physical attraction matters. Not just initially, but throughout the marriage.

The data: Beauty

• 35% of African respondents considered beauty as essential

• 33% of American respondents said the same

The data: Height

• 21% of African respondents considered height compatibility essential

• 27% of American respondents said the same

However, what constitutes attraction varies enormously across cultures:

• Height preferences (strong in some cultures, irrelevant in others)

• Body type ideals

• Skin colour preferences

• Facial features and beauty standards

• Overall physical chemistry and sexual compatibility

The balance:

• Physical attraction and sexual chemistry should be present

• But they shouldn't be the primary or only factor

• Attraction can deepen as emotional intimacy grows

• Bodies change with age, health, childbirth—attraction must evolve beyond the superficial

Ask yourself:

• Am I physically attracted to this person?

• Do we have chemistry?

• Am I attracted to who they are or just how they look?

• Can I imagine still being attracted to them as we both age?

8. Religious Compatibility

We touched on this in the previous chapter and it is also fully covered in Chapter 10, but it deserves a mention here as a selection factor. My survey revealed that religious compatibility ranked among the top three factors for respondents who considered themselves religious.

For religious people, be extremely careful about marrying someone who doesn't share your faith. The statistics show these marriages face significantly higher failure rates. If you choose to proceed, get extensive counselling beforehand and have explicit, detailed agreements about practice and children.

Ranking Exercise: What Really Matters To You?

Now that we've explored all eight factors, rank them in order of importance to you:

1. ____
2. ____
3. ____
4. ____
5. ____
6. ____
7. ____
8. ____

Then, have your partner (or potential partner) rank them separately. Compare your lists. Where do you align? Where do you differ? Those differences deserve deep conversation.

Comparative Analysis: USA Vs. Africa

When I compiled my survey data, clear patterns emerged in how Americans and Africans weighted these factors differently:

Africans prioritized:
1. Financial stability
2. Religious compatibility
3. Education level
4. Love
5. Family background

Americans prioritized:
1. Love and emotional connection
2. Financial stability
3. Education level

Neither ranking is "right" or "wrong." They reflect different cultural realities, values, and social structures. What's fascinating is what happens when people from these different cultural frameworks marry—which factors win? How do couples bridge these different priority systems?

In my own cross-cultural marriage, we had to navigate my African cultural conditioning (which prioritized duty, family, and practical considerations) with my wife's expectations (which emphasized emotional connection, individual fulfilment, and companionship). We've learned to honour both frameworks, taking the best from each tradition.

The Danger Of Ignoring Any Factor

Here's what I learned from my research: While you don't need perfection in all eight areas, ignoring any factor completely often creates problems later. The man who married for love alone without considering financial compatibility found himself constantly fighting about money. The woman who married for security without genuine attraction found herself vulnerable to affairs. The couple who had everything except religious compatibility struggled for years over how to raise their children.

As outlined in Chapter 3, you must decide which factors are non-negotiable for you—but don't completely dismiss the others. They all matter to some degree.

Red Flags And Deal-breakers

As you evaluate potential partners against these eight factors, watch for:

Red Flag: Significant misalignment in top three priorities

Example: You ranked financial stability #2; they ranked it #8 and have massive debt they're unconcerned about

Red Flag: Complete inability to discuss a factor

Example: They shut down every conversation about religion or family background

Red Flag: Expecting you to change fundamental aspects of who you are

Example: "Once we're married, you'll become more religious/less religious/more ambitious/less career-focused"

Red Flag: Family's complete rejection of the relationship

Example: Their family refuses to meet you or threatens disownment (This isn't always a deal-breaker, but it requires serious consideration)

Red Flag: You don't respect them in one or more key areas

Example: You think they're physically attractive but intellectually boring, or you admire their intelligence but have no physical chemistry

The Myth Of The Perfect Match

After all this analysis, let me be clear: There is no perfect partner who scores 10/10 in all eight categories. If you wait for perfection, you'll wait forever.

What you're looking for is:
- Strength in the areas most important to you
- "Good enough" in the areas less critical
- Shared willingness to grow and adapt
- Problems you can live with
- Differences that enrich rather than divide

Practical Application

Before moving forward in your relationship:

1. Complete the ranking exercise honestly

2. Have your partner do the same

3. Compare and discuss differences

4. Identify where you have strengths and where you have challenges

5. Decide together: Are the challenges manageable? Are the strengths

sufficient?

6. Get input from trusted mentors who know you both

7. Be willing to walk away if the misalignment is too significant

Remember: It's better to be single than to be in a mismatched marriage. The pain of loneliness is temporary. The pain of a fundamentally incompatible marriage can last decades.

Reflection & Assessment

Personal Reflection

Which compatibility factors mattered most to me at the time?
Which did I underestimate or overlook?

Partner Dialogue

Where are we most aligned?
Where are we most mismatched?

Reality Check

For each area, mark one: Aligned / Somewhat Aligned / Misaligned

Communication
Values
Finances
Faith or belief system
Family expectations

Looking Forward

In the next chapter, we'll explore the courtship period—how to use your dating time to thoroughly evaluate these eight factors and make a wise decision about commitment. Because choosing your partner is arguably the most important decision you'll ever make, second only to your relationship with God (if you're religious). Take it seriously. Take your time. And choose well. Your future self will thank you.

Scan this code for a short reflection related to Part I.

PART II - THE JOURNEY: COURTSHIP TO COMMITMENT

The transition from courtship to marriage involves navigating expectations that differ significantly between cultures. Our survey reveals that family background matters far more in African partner selection (52% agreement) than in American contexts (31%). This suggests African couples face more intensive family scrutiny during courtship, while American couples may enjoy greater independence but potentially less family support.

Interestingly, age difference considerations show similar patterns: 48% of African and 36% of American respondents consider age gaps important. This similarity suggests cross-cultural recognition that age compatibility affects relationship dynamics, though neither culture treats it as a deal-breaker.

The survey's employment data reveals both populations are primarily composed of working adults (71% Africa, 64% USA), suggesting that economic productivity and relationship readiness often coincide. Single respondents—comprising 37% of African and 31% of American samples—provide insight into pre-marriage attitudes, showing similar patterns to their married counterparts in what they value.

Pause for Reflection

This part of *The Second Bridge* is designed to be read as a whole. Before moving to the next section, you are invited to pause and reflect on the ideas explored across all the chapters in this part.

A short reflection questionnaire is available to help you assess insights, patterns, and areas for growth.

Please complete the questionnaire only after reading all chapters in this part. (Scan the code at the end of this section to access the reflection.)

THE SECOND BRIDGE

CHAPTER 5: THE COURTSHIP PERIOD

*The questions you avoid before marriage become the conflicts
you cannot escape after.*

Courtship is where theory becomes reality. You can know all eight factors to consider in choosing a partner, but courtship is where you discover whether the person in front of you actually possesses the qualities you're seeking—or whether they're simply showing you what you want to see.

In this chapter, we'll explore how to approach courtship strategically while maintaining authenticity, how long it should last, what questions you must ask, and how to recognize when you've found the right person—or when you need to walk away.

The Purpose Of Courtship

Let me start with something that might surprise you: The primary purpose of courtship is not to fall deeper in love. It's to gather information. "But that sounds so unromantic!" I hear you protesting. Yet this mindset saved me from at least one marriage and has helped countless couples.

Here's the truth: Romantic feelings create a kind of temporary insanity. Brain scans show that early romantic love activates the same regions associated with cocaine use. You're literally high on your own neurochemicals. In this state, you cannot think clearly about whether this person is a good long-term partner.

Courtship exists to:

1. Observe your potential partner in various situations
2. Meet and assess their family, friends, and community
3. Discuss expectations, values, and life goals
4. Discover how they handle stress, conflict, and disappointment
5. Evaluate compatibility across all eight factors we discussed
6. Test whether your initial attraction has substance beneath it
7. Give trusted advisors time to offer perspective

One African tradition I deeply appreciate is the involvement of families in courtship. While Americans often see this as intrusive, there's wisdom in having people who love you but aren't intoxicated by romantic feelings observe your potential partner with clearer eyes. Someone once said: "When you're choosing a wife, you're drunk. Let people who are sober help you decide." This might sound harsh, but it's accurate.

How Long Should Courtship Last?

We should avoid generalizations. What matters more than duration is intentionality. A couple who dates for 18 months while actively assessing compatibility, discussing difficult topics, and introducing each other to family and community is better prepared than a couple who dates for five years without having serious conversations.

The Key Questions: Are you actively moving toward a decision, or are you just letting time pass?

What To Observe During Courtship

Courtship is an extended observation period. Here's what to pay attention to:

1. How They Handle Stress

Anyone can be pleasant when life is easy. How do they respond when:

- Work is demanding
- They're sick or exhausted
- Plans go wrong
- They're disappointed or frustrated
- They receive criticism
- They don't get their way

I have watched my partner navigate a family crisis. The crisis was heart-breaking, but how she handled it—with grace, strength, and compassion—showed me who she truly was.

2. How They Treat Service Workers

This sounds like a cliché, but it's accurate: Watch how your partner treats waiters, janitors, cashiers, and others in service positions. How someone treats people who can do nothing for them reveals character.

3. Their Relationship with Family

You're not just marrying an individual; you're joining their family system. During courtship, observe:

- How they speak about family members (with respect or contempt?)
- How they respond to family requests and obligations
- Whether they have healthy boundaries or are enmeshed

• How their family treats them and treats you
• Family dysfunction (addiction, abuse, mental illness) and whether they've addressed it
Red flags:
• Speaking disrespectfully about parents (especially the parent of the same gender—this may predict how they'll eventually treat you)
• Complete inability to say no to family requests
• Hiding you from family or refusing to introduce you
• Family's open hostility toward you
• Unresolved trauma or dysfunction that they refuse to address
4. How They Handle Money
We've discussed financial compatibility, but during courtship, observe actual behaviours:
• Do they pay bills on time?
• Do they live within their means?
• How do they spend money—impulsively or thoughtfully?
• Do they have a budget and financial plan?
• How do they respond to financial setbacks?
• Are they generous or stingy?
• Do they hide financial information or are they transparent?
5. How They Fight
Conflict is inevitable in any relationship. During courtship, you'll disagree—hopefully about something minor. This is actually a gift because it reveals conflict patterns.
Healthy conflict includes:
• Expressing disagreement respectfully
• Listening to understand, not just to rebut
• Taking breaks if emotions escalate
• Apologizing and forgiving
• Finding compromise
• Not bringing up past issues
• No name-calling, contempt, or physical aggression
Unhealthy patterns include:
• Silent treatment or stonewalling
• Yelling, name-calling, or contempt
• Bringing up every past mistake
• Refusing to apologize or accept apologies
• Always needing to "win"
• Physical intimidation
• Making threats

If you see unhealthy patterns during courtship—when you're both on your best behaviour—they will only worsen after marriage. This is not the time to ignore red flags hoping they'll change.

6. Their Spiritual Life

For religious people, observe not just stated beliefs but actual practices:

• Do they attend services regularly?
• Do they pray or engage in spiritual practices?
• How do they speak about God/faith?
• Do their actions align with their stated values?
• Are they growing spiritually or stagnant?
• Is their faith a source of peace or anxiety?

I've known people who claimed strong faith but whose lives showed no evidence of it. I've also known people whose faith transformed everything they did. During courtship, you discover which kind of person you're dealing with.

7. Their Friendships

Show me your friends, and I'll show you your future. During courtship, pay attention to:

• Do they have long-term friendships?
• How do they speak about friends?
• Are their friends people of character?
• Do their friends respect you?
• How do they balance friendship with your relationship? Someone with no long-term friends is a major red flag. Inability to maintain friendships often indicates inability to maintain marriages.

8. How They Treat You

This seems obvious, but many people ignore poor treatment during courtship:

• Do they respect your boundaries?
• Do they listen when you express concerns?
• Do they prioritize your needs alongside their own?
• Do you feel cherished and valued?
• Are they proud of you or embarrassed by you?
• Do they support your goals and dreams?

If someone treats you poorly while trying to win you, they'll treat you worse after they've secured you. Believe them when they show you who they are.

Essential Conversations

Beyond observation, courtship must include explicit conversations about:

Children:
- Do you both want children?
- If yes, how many and when?
- How will you handle infertility?
- What parenting approach will you take?
- How will you discipline children?

Finances:
- What are current debts and assets?
- How will finances be managed?
- What are career ambitions?
- What lifestyle do you expect?
- What financial obligations exist to extended family?

Religion:
- What do you believe?
- How will you practice faith together?
- Where will you worship?
- How will you raise children spiritually?

Extended Family:
- What obligations do you have to family?
- How much will family be involved in your lives?
- Where will you live in relation to family?
- How will you handle family conflicts?

Life Vision:
- Where do you want to live?
- What career paths will you pursue?
- What does your ideal life look like in 10, 20, 30 years?
- What legacy do you want to leave?

Past Relationships:
- What past relationships have you had?
- What did you learn from them?
- Are there any ongoing connections to exes?
- Have there been any abusive relationships?

Deal Breakers:
- What would cause you to leave the marriage?
- What behaviours are unacceptable?
- Where are you unwilling to compromise?

These conversations aren't romantic, but they're essential. If you can't have difficult conversations during courtship, you certainly won't be able to have them during marriage.

The Authenticity Challenge

Here's the courtship paradox: You need to observe who your partner truly is, but both of you are naturally putting your best foot forward. How do you see beneath the performance?

Time is your friend. Masks slip eventually. The person who is unfailingly patient for three months might show frustration by month six. The person who seems financially responsible might reveal concerning spending by month nine.

Meet their people. Talk to their friends, family, co-workers. You'll hear stories and see patterns. Ask questions like: "What's [partner] like when they're stressed?" or "Can you tell me about a time when [partner] faced a disappointment?"

Create varied experiences. Don't just go on fancy dates. Travel together (nothing reveals character like travel problems). Serve together at a charity. Attend a funeral or support someone in crisis together. Normal dates show you Sunday-best behaviour. Varied experiences show you reality.

Trust your instincts. If something feels off, it probably is. Don't ignore that inner voice telling you something isn't right just because you want the relationship to work.

My Courtship Mistakes

When I met my former wife, we did not discuss any of the above. I thought I could handle any challenge we might face because I am a very patient person and can adapt. Looking back, I can see we were fundamentally incompatible, but I was too young and too invested to admit it. We differed on:

- The number of children (I wanted less, she wanted more)
- Where to live (she wanted to stay in one city; I knew my career would require mobility)
- Religious practice (I wanted to grow spiritually; she was comfortable with nominalism)
- Financial approach (she was a spender; I was a saver)
- Growth mindset (I had a growth mindset and she didn't)

After we got married, we were comfortable. We knew each other's routines. Breaking up seemed harder than staying together.

When we finally broke up (painfully, messily), I was devastated. But, I recognized it as the best thing that could have happened. I was finally free to find someone actually compatible.

When I met my current wife, the difference was immediately apparent. Our courtship lasted four months—long enough to be sure, short enough that we weren't wasting time. We had difficult conversations early. We observed each other in various situations. We introduced each other to family and friends. We discussed our eight factors openly.

And when challenges arose after marriage (and they did), we had a foundation of compatibility and honest communication that allowed us to navigate them together.

When To End A Courtship

This is perhaps the most important decision: recognizing when a relationship shouldn't proceed to marriage. Here are clear indicators:
End it if:
- You don't respect them
- They don't respect you
- You're trying to change fundamental aspects of who they are
- They're trying to change fundamental aspects of who you are
- You have completely different life visions
- They show patterns of abuse, addiction, or untreated mental. illness
- Your core values are incompatible
- You're staying out of fear (of being alone, of disappointing others, of wasted time)
- Trusted advisors unanimously warn you against the marriage
- You're hoping they'll change after marriage

That last point deserves emphasis: People do not change because they get married. If someone is controlling, selfish, irresponsible, or unkind during courtship, marriage will amplify these traits, not eliminate them.

The sunk cost fallacy destroys lives. "But we've been together for five years!" Yes, and do you want to waste five more? Fifty more? Better to end it now than divorce later.

When To Move Forward

Conversely, here are indicators that you should move toward marriage:
Move forward if:
- You respect and admire them
- You share core values and life vision
- You've observed them in varied situations and like what you've seen
- You've had difficult conversations and resolved conflicts well
- Your families and communities support the relationship
- You're compatible across most of the eight factors
- You feel peaceful about the decision (not just excited, but peaceful)
- You can imagine navigating life's challenges together
- You bring out the best in better in each other
- You're ready for the commitment marriage requires

Notice I didn't say "if you can't imagine life without them" or "if you're madly in love." Those feelings are wonderful but insufficient. What matters more is whether you have a solid foundation for a lifelong partnership.

Practical Steps Before Engagement

If you're considering engagement, take these final steps:

1. Complete a premarital assessment tool such as the one in this book.

2. Attend premarital counselling with a licensed Counsellor or experienced pastoral Counsellor

3. Spend significant time with each other's families

4. Have a professional financial planning conversation together

5. Discuss your assessment tool results and any red flags honestly

6. Ask trusted mentors for honest feedback about the relationship

7. If religious, pray extensively about the decision

8. Give yourselves permission to end it if significant problems emerge

These steps aren't guarantees, but they significantly increase your odds of a successful marriage.

Reflection & Assessment

Personal Reflection
Did I use courtship to observe or to impress?
What truths emerged early that I chose to ignore?
Partner Dialogue
What did we learn about each other early on?
What important conversations did we avoid?
Reality Check: Tick all that apply:
☐ We asked difficult questions early

☐ We avoided uncomfortable truths

☐ We rushed commitment

The Bottom Line

Courtship is your opportunity to make the most important decision of your life with as much information and wisdom as possible. Don't rush it. Don't ignore red flags. Don't let pressure from others override your better judgment.

But also, don't let fear prevent you from committing when you've found someone genuinely compatible. Perfect partners don't exist. Good enough partners with whom you can build something beautiful absolutely do.

In the next chapter, we'll discuss marriage arrangements—the practical and ceremonial aspects of transitioning from courtship to commitment. But before we move forward, make sure you've completed the work of courtship thoroughly. Your future self—and your future marriage—will thank you.

CHAPTER 6: MARRIAGE ARRANGEMENTS

Commitment without evaluation is hope disguised as preparation.

Courtship has reached its natural conclusion. You've observed each other in various situations, had the difficult conversations, met each other's families, and decided you want to build a life together. Now comes the practical reality: How do you actually get married? This chapter explores the marriage arrangement process—from traditional ceremonies to modern weddings, from family negotiations to personal choices, and from the money discussions that nobody wants to have to the compromises that make everything possible.

The Marriage Arrangement Spectrum

Marriage arrangements exist on a spectrum from completely arranged (where families choose partners with minimal input from the couple) to completely autonomous (where the couple makes all decisions independently). Most marriages fall somewhere in between, influenced by culture, religion, family dynamics, and personal preferences.

Growing up, I watched elaborate marriage arrangements that involved extensive family negotiations. Bride price discussions, family investigations into each other's backgrounds (See Chapter 2), and ceremonial protocols that had been followed for generations—these weren't just traditions, they were the way marriages happened.

In other cultures, couples often planned weddings with minimal family input, sometimes not even informing parents until arrangements were finalized. The truth, as usual, lies in nuance. Both extremes have problems. Completely arranged marriages can ignore compatibility and individual desires. Completely autonomous arrangements can dismiss valuable family wisdom and create unnecessary family conflict.

The Traditional African Approach

Let me describe how marriage arrangements worked in a typical African community, because understanding traditional approaches helps us evaluate modern alternatives.

Stage 1: Family Investigation

Once a man decided to marry a woman (or more traditionally, once families identified a potential match), both families conducted investigations:

- What is the family's reputation in the community?
- Are there histories of mental illness, violence, or serious hereditary diseases?
- How do they treat their own family members?
- What are their financial circumstances?
- What is their standing in the community?

Americans often find this intrusive. But consider: You're joining families, not just individuals. Wouldn't you want to know if your potential in-laws have a pattern of interfering in marriages, or if there's addiction running through the family? These are safety measures built into marriage institutions to ensure continuous functional society.

During my first marriage, some of my family members warned me of a particular pattern that is prevalent in the family of my intended wife, and some of them advised against the marriage which I ignored. There is a Yoruba (a tribe in Nigeria) adage that says: "The word of elders that do not come to pass in the morning will come to pass at night." That was exactly what happened 35 years later.

Stage 2: Formal Introduction

If investigations proved satisfactory, the man's family formally visited the woman's family to declare intentions. This wasn't a small affair—extended family members attended, gifts were presented, and respect was shown through elaborate protocols. Three of my four children have passed through this process without exception. This process was followed in my second marriage.

The woman's family in some cases do not immediately accept the marriage proposal. They would say they needed time to "consider" and "pray about" the proposal. This wasn't game-playing; it was demonstrating that their daughter was valuable and the decision weighty.

Stage 3: Bride Price Negotiation

Here's where Western countries get most uncomfortable: bride price. Let me clarify what it is and isn't. Bride price is NOT selling a woman. It's a demonstration that:
- The man and his family value the woman
- They have resources to care for her
- They understand marriage creates obligations
- They're willing to make sacrifices
- The families are now connected

Bride price might include livestock, money, gifts for the bride's mother and extended family, and contributions to family needs. In some Nigerian cultures, the amount reflected the bride's educational level, character, and family status.

Stage 4: Traditional and Religious Ceremonies

Most traditional African marriages involve multiple ceremonies:
- Traditional ceremony in the bride's community
- Traditional ceremony in the groom's community
- Religious ceremony (Christian, Muslim, or indigenous)
- Legal registration

Each ceremony had significance. The traditional ceremonies honoured ancestors and cultural identity. The religious ceremony sought divine blessing. The legal registration provided governmental protection.

These multiple ceremonies weren't redundant—they recognized that marriage exists in multiple dimensions: personal, familial, spiritual, communal, and legal.

The Modern Western countries' Approach

Western countries' marriage arrangements look dramatically different, shaped by individualism, mobility, and different family structures.

Stage 1: The Proposal

In Western culture, the man typically proposes to the woman (though this is slowly changing). The proposal has become increasingly elaborate—flash mobs, destination proposals, carefully orchestrated surprises. Instagram and TikTok have turned proposals into performance art.

It is not unusual for a fiancé to propose at home, just the two of them, with a modest ring. This happens in some cases due to financial challenges or family disapproval. The pressure to create a proposal story worth posting has created anxiety and expense that have nothing to do with the actual relationship.

Stage 2: Announcing to Families

Often, Western countries' couples announce their engagement to their families after the fact. Some men maintain the tradition of asking the woman's father for permission, but this is becoming less common.

The asking-permission tradition has problems (it can treat women as property to be transferred), but the underlying principle—respecting family connections and seeking blessing—has value.

Stage 3: Wedding Planning

This is where Western countries' marriage arrangements get complicated. Who plans the wedding? Who pays for it? Whose vision prevails? Traditional etiquette said the bride's family paid for the wedding, but this tradition has largely collapsed as weddings have become more expensive and families more diverse.

Stage 4: The Ceremony

Western weddings have become elaborate productions. Couples spend months planning details that will be experienced for a few hours. Compare this to many traditional African ceremonies, which cost less but involved entire communities and lasted days. Neither approach is inherently superior, but both reveal values: Western countries prioritize individual expression and aesthetic perfection; Africans prioritize community participation and cultural continuity. However, this is also changing gradually in Africa as couples now copy the Western countries' approach to weddings due to the influence of media media.

Navigating Cross-Cultural Marriage Arrangements

When two different cultural traditions collide, marriage arrangements become particularly complex which require negotiations that include:

- Which traditional ceremonies to include
- How to meet both families' expectations
- Where to hold ceremonies
- Who to invite
- How much to spend
- What compromises were acceptable

Mistakes are made, feelings are hurt, and a lot of money spent trying to please everyone. For these reasons, it is important to:

1. Establish clearer boundaries earlier

Any attempt to please everyone can be exhausting and is impossible.

2. Be more explicit about budget

Not to allow family expectations drive spending beyond what is affordable.

3. Prioritize what actually matter to the couple

Include traditions that are meaningful to both couples and not to the families.

4. Be more willing to disappoint people

The truth is that you cannot please everyone. Trying to do so pleases no one, including yourselves.

Essential Conversations Before Arrangements Begin

Couples must discuss and agree on these issues before beginning marriage arrangements:

Budget and Financial Responsibility

Agree on:

• Maximum total budget

• Who will pay for what

• Whether you'll accept family financial contributions (and what strings might be attached)

• What you'll do if costs exceed budget

• How you'll handle family pressure to spend more

Have the money conversation first, before looking at venues or trying on dresses.

Decision-Making Authority

Decide:

• Who makes final decisions (couple? families? some combination?)

• How you'll handle disagreements]

• What role each family will play

• What happens when families' desires conflict with yours

• How you'll communicate boundaries to families

The key question: Are you planning your wedding, or are you planning your families' wedding?

Cultural and Religious Elements

Discuss:

• Which cultural traditions you'll honour

• Which you'll modify or skip

• How you'll blend different traditions

• What religious elements you'll include
• How you'll handle family objections to your choices

For interfaith or cross-cultural couples, this is especially critical. You're not just planning a wedding—you're establishing patterns for how you'll navigate cultural and religious differences throughout your marriage.

Guest List Philosophy

Agree on:

• Approximate guest count
• Balance between families
• Whether you'll invite people you don't know to please families
• How to handle family pressure to invite more people
• What to do if you want a small wedding but families want large

Timeline and Urgency

Discuss:

• How long before the wedding
• Whether there's any rush (pregnancy, military deployment, immigration issues)
• How much planning time you need
• What happens if you need to postpone

Common Marriage Arrangement Conflicts

Let me walk you through the most common conflicts and how to navigate them:

Conflict 1: Traditional vs. Modern

One partner wants traditional ceremonies honouring cultural heritage; the other wants a modern, simplified approach.

Solution: Identify which traditional elements are truly meaningful vs. which are just "what's done." Keep what matters, simplify what doesn't. Consider having a small traditional ceremony for family and a separate modern celebration for friends.

Conflict 2: Religious Differences

Partners from different faiths struggle with which religious official to use, which traditions to include, whose religious community to honour.

Solution: This should be addressed during courtship. If you reached marriage arrangements without resolving religious differences, postpone until you do. Religious conflicts only intensify after marriage.

Conflict 3: Size and Budget

One partner/family wants large, expensive celebration; the other wants small, simple, affordable.

Solution: Remember that the wedding is one day, but the marriage lasts decades. Don't start your marriage in debt for a party. If families want larger celebrations, they can fund them—but maintain final decision-making authority.

Conflict 4: Family Involvement vs. Couple Autonomy

Families feel entitled to make decisions; couple wants independence.

Solution: Early, clear communication about boundaries. "We value your input and want your blessing, but we're making final decisions. We'll share our plans with you, but we're not asking permission." Then enforce those boundaries consistently.

Conflict 5: Cultural Disconnection

Cross-cultural couples face families who don't understand or value each other's traditions.

Solution: Education and translation. Help each family understand the significance of the other's traditions. Find common ground. Create new traditions that honour both heritages.

The Bride Price Conversation For Cross-Cultural Couples

This deserves special attention because it creates enormous conflict in African-Western marriages. In some cases, the African family expect bride price and the Western partner (or their family) found the concept offensive. The Western family often views it as "buying" a daughter; the African family views refusal as profound disrespect suggesting the bride has no value. Here's how to navigate this:

For the African Partner:

• Explain the cultural significance to your Western partner and their family
  • Clarify that it's symbolic, not transactional
  • Be willing to modify the practice to fit new cultural context
  • Don't let it become a financial burden that damages the marriage before it begins

For the Western Partner:

• Approach with cultural humility rather than judgment
  • Recognize that your culture has its own symbolic (and expensive) marriage traditions

• Consider what bride price means to your partner's family identity
• Find compromises that honour the spirit without excessive expense

For Both:
• Discuss this early, not during wedding planning
• Set clear limits on amount
• Frame it as honouring tradition, not obligation
• Be willing to educate both families about the compromise you've reached

Practical Advice For Marriage Arrangements

Here are practical steps:

1. Start with Private Agreement

Before involving families, agree privately on:
• Budget
• Decision-making process
• Non-negotiables
• Timeline
• Vision for the ceremony

2. Communicate Clearly with Families

Present your decisions as information, not requests for permission. "We've decided to…….." not "What do you think about…..."

3. Be Willing to Compromise on Secondary Issues

Save your firm boundaries for what truly matters. If your mother-in-law desperately wants to choose bridesmaid dresses and you don't care, let her. Save your "no" for issues that matter to you.

4. Keep Perspective

The wedding is one day. The marriage is (hopefully) decades. Don't damage your relationship or family relationships over flower arrangements or invitation fonts.

5. Build in Buffer

Expect conflicts. Expect delays. Expect some things to go wrong. Plan and budget with cushion for the unexpected.

6. Consider Alternative Approaches

Some couples are choosing:
• Destination weddings (smaller, more intimate, less family interference)
• Courthouse weddings followed by separate celebrations
• Long engagements with multiple smaller ceremonies in different locations

• Skipping traditional weddings entirely

None of these is wrong. Choose what serves your relationship and values.

7. Get Help

Consider hiring a wedding planner, not just for logistics but as a buffer between you and family expectations. Good planners are experts at managing family dynamics while protecting couple's vision.

The Deeper Purpose

Before we move to the next chapter, let me remind you of something crucial: Marriage arrangements are about more than planning a party. How you navigate the marriage arrangement process reveals and shapes your relationship:

• Can you make decisions together under pressure?
• Can you maintain boundaries with families?
• Can you compromise with each other?
• Can you handle conflict productively?
• Can you keep perspective on what matters?

If you cannot navigate wedding planning successfully, how will you navigate buying a house, raising children, or handling financial crises? The marriage arrangement process is your first major test as a couple. Pass it by:

• Communicating clearly
• Respecting each other's values
• Maintaining united front with families
• Keeping focus on your relationship, not just the event
• Demonstrating financial responsibility
• Showing flexibility and humour when things go wrong

Do this well, and you're building skills that will serve your marriage for decades.

Reflection & Assessment

Personal Reflection

How did culture, family, or religion influence our marriage decisions?

Did tradition strengthen or strain our union?

Partner Dialogue

Which expectations came from family rather than us?

What would we do differently today?

Reality Check Rate from 1–5:
Our marriage structure reflects our shared values

Looking Ahead

The wedding day will come and go, photographed and remembered but ultimately just the beginning. In the next chapter, we'll discuss what follows: early in marriage, the adjustment period, and the first year challenges that test even the strongest relationships.

But first, you have to get through the marriage arrangements. Do so with wisdom, grace, and a clear focus on what truly matters: not the perfect party, but the lasting partnership you're building.

CHAPTER 7: EARLY IN MARRIAGE

Marriage is not a destination; it is a structure that must be reinforced daily.

The Adjustment Phase

The wedding is over. The honeymoon has ended. You're home, and suddenly you're living with this person every single day. Welcome to early in marriage—the adjustment phase that nobody warns you about adequately.

In this chapter, we'll explore the first year of marriage, why it's so challenging, what common surprises await you, and how to navigate this critical period without letting it damage your relationship before it truly begins.

The Reality Nobody Mentions

• You wished someone told you marriage was harder than expected

• You wished you knew disagreement will be more than during courtship

• You would question yourself at some point whether you'd made the right choice

• You wished someone had prepared you better

• That you would be glad you married your spouse despite the challenges

The early difficulty in the marriage doesn't mean you married the wrong person—it means you're adjusting to a profound life change, and making adjustment is inherently uncomfortable.

The Five Major Adjustments

Early in the marriage requires adjustment in five major areas:

1. Daily Living Habits

You're not just sharing space—you're synchronizing life rhythms:

Morning routines (early riser vs. night owl)

Cleanliness standards (spotless vs. "clean enough")

Food preferences and cooking habits

Temperature preferences (thermostat wars)
Noise tolerance
Sleep schedules and bedroom environment
Bathroom routines and timing
How you spend free time

These sound trivial until you're living them. Disagreement could occur over thermostat settings—by one person wanting it at 65°F, the other wanting 74°F. This isn't really about temperature; it is about whether each person's comfort mattered to the other.

Practical potential conflicts are:

• "He leaves wet towels on the floor every single day."

• "She takes 45-minute showers, and we have one bathroom."

• "He goes to bed at 9 PM; I'm a night person. We never see each other."

• "She's a slob, and I need order. Our apartment is a constant negotiation."

Solution: Discuss daily habits before marriage, but accept that reality will differ from what you imagined. Focus on identifying which habits truly matter to you (deal-breakers) vs. which are just different from your preference (annoying but tolerable). Compromise on the annoying; insist on boundaries for the deal-breakers.

2. Financial Integration

Remember that 48% of Americans and 41% of Africans in our survey said finances were critical to marriage? The first year is when this becomes viscerally real. You must decide:

• Joint accounts, separate accounts, or hybrid?

• Who pays which bills?

• How much autonomy does each person have?

• What purchases require discussion?

• How to handle different earning levels

• How to manage debt brought into marriage

• Savings goals and priorities

For instance, one could make twice what the other makes which could result on the assumption that the one that makes more should make financial decisions whilst this other believes they should have equal say regardless of who earned more. This could result in constant disagreement about money that might require discussion instead of making assumptions. The first year often brings financial surprises:

• Hidden debts revealed

• Different spending patterns causing conflict

• Family financial obligations emerging

• Unexpected expenses (car repair, medical bills, job loss)
• Shock at the cost of running a household

Solution: Have explicit financial meetings. Weekly at first, then monthly as you develop systems. Review all accounts together. Create budget together. Discuss every purchase over a certain amount (agree on the threshold). Be completely transparent about debts, family obligations, and spending.

3. Sexual Adjustment

Whether you had sex before marriage or waited, married sexual intimacy differs from dating physical affection. Early marriage requires learning:

• Each other's actual desires and preferences (not what you assumed)
• How to communicate about sex clearly
• How to navigate different desire levels
• How fatigue, stress, and schedules affect intimacy
• What to do when one person wants sex and the other doesn't
• How to maintain romance amid daily life pressures

Possible areas of disagreement are:
• Mismatched desire levels
• Different expectations about frequency
• Difficulty communicating about preferences
• Stress and exhaustion affecting intimacy
• Body image concerns
• Religious guilt (for those who waited until marriage)
• Past trauma affecting current intimacy

Couples who both waited until marriage could on the wedding night become nervous and feel awkward. It might take months before adjustment to enjoyable sex rather than stressful. Expect a learning curve. Another example could be couples who during dating, couldn't keep their hands off each other and losing interest after the wedding leading to one party feeling rejected and unattractive. A discussion could lead to the realisation that it is as a result of work and stress and not personal. Communication about intimacy becomes essential to a successful love life. A married African female in our survey said:

"He is not romantic."

Solution: Talk about sex explicitly. Don't assume your partner knows what you want or how you feel. Schedule intimacy if necessary (yes, this can be romantic—it shows you're prioritizing each other). If problems persist beyond a few months, see a Counsellor who specializes in sexual intimacy. Don't let this fester.

4. Family Boundary Setting

In Africa, when you enter into a marriage relationship, you are not only marrying your spouse, you marry the whole family (See Chapter 2). Almost everybody would like to have a say in your affairs. First-year conflicts often involve:

- How often to visit parents
- How much to share with parents about your marriage
- Whether parents can drop by unannounced
- How involved parents should be in decisions
- How to split holidays between families
- Whether to live near family or move away
- How to handle family criticism of your spouse

In African culture, mother in-laws play key role in marriages ranging from visit expectation, frequency of calls, opinions about how the wife cooked, cleaned, dressed. Setting boundaries could lead to mother in-laws getting hurt.

An instance is where one of the spouses tells their mother everything—every argument had, every problem and the mother calls the other spouse to lecture about dos and don'ts in marriage making them feel like there is no privacy in the marriage. This happens when one or both spouses are close to their mother.

Solution: Discuss family boundaries explicitly before marriage, then enforce them consistently. You're building a new family unit—your marriage is now your primary family. Honour your parents, but prioritize your spouse. Be willing to disappoint parents to protect your marriage. Present united front—never let family play you against each other.

5. Identity Integration

This is the subtlest but perhaps deepest adjustment: integrating your individual identity with your identity as "married person." Questions arise:

- How much independence do I maintain?
- What friendships continue, and how?
- Do I need permission or just need to inform?
- How much time alone is acceptable?
- What activities do we do separately vs. together?
- How much should I consider my spouse before making decisions?

A situation where one of the partners was used to making decisions independently—where to go, what to do, when to do it and suddenly had to consider someone else's preferences, schedule, and feelings could feel suffocating sometimes. Marriage doesn't mean losing yourself, but it does mean considering someone else in your decisions.

An Uber driver once narrated to me how his spouse after marriage decided to go on a cruise with others girls without him. He was livid and wanted my advice. The spouse was used to "hanging out with the girls" before they got married as she had a good job and could afford it. This was not discussed before they got married. My question to him was "What was he expecting?" to which he had no answer. That ended the conversation.

A man whose buddies expected him to keep hanging out with them like he did before he got married while his wife is expecting him to spend most free time with her leading to him feeling torn between his old life and the new life. This could result in a fight between him and his wife. The man would have to create a new balance by spending some time with friends, more time with his wife, and some time alone.

Solution: Discuss expectations about independence, time alone, friendships, and activities. Recognize that you're both learning a new dance—sometimes you'll step on each other's toes. Give each other grace. Adjust as you learn what works for your unique relationship. Always remember the Three Pillars in conflict resolution (See Chapter 1)

The First Major Fight

Almost every couple has one—the fight that's disproportionately intense, often about something seemingly minor. Common triggers are:
- Household chores
- Money/spending
- Family interference
- Sex/intimacy
- Friends/social life

But here's what I learned: The trigger isn't really what the fight is about. Your first major fight is usually about power, respect, and how you'll handle conflict. You're testing:
- Will you hear me?
- Will you respect my needs?
- Can I be angry without being abandoned?
- How will we resolve differences?
- Is it safe to disagree?

A fight could occur over meal where one spouse wants to have chicken and the other steak which could escalate into massive argument. But really, the fight could be about whether one spouse preferences mattered, whether to ask before making decisions, and whether the other's effort is appreciated. The meal is just the vehicle.

How To Fight Well Early In The Marriage

Since conflict is inevitable, learn to fight productively:

DO:
- Use "I feel" statements instead of "You always/never"
- Take breaks if emotions escalate
- Listen to understand, not to win
- Acknowledge valid points your partner makes
- Apologize when you're wrong
- Focus on the specific issue at hand
- Assume good intentions

DON'T:
- Bring up past issues
- Call names or show contempt
- Threaten divorce
- Involve family/friends in your fights
- Go to bed angry if you can resolve it
- Give silent treatment
- Keep score

A "fight fair" agreement could be:
- No fighting when tired, hungry, or drunk
- No fighting in public
- Call time-outs if too emotional
- Return to discussion within 24 hours
- End fights with physical reconnection (hug, hold hands)

This structure helps navigate early marriage conflicts without lasting damage.

Common First-Year Surprises

Let me share what most couples wish they'd known:

Surprise 1: Marriage doesn't fix problems

The thought that marriage would make you more secure, less jealous, more committed. Instead, insecurities could intensify. Understand that marriage doesn't fix issues.

Surprise 2: You can love someone and still want space

Feeling guilty for wanting alone time, thinking that marriage meant wanting to be together constantly. Learn to love deeply and still have some time alone.

Surprise 3: Household labour is never equally distributed

"We both work full-time, but somehow I still do 80% of housework chores." Engage and work it out.

Surprise 4: You'll see your partner at their worst

"Dating shows you Sunday-best behaviour. Marriage shows you sick, exhausted, stressed, angry, scared, and petty." It's less romantic and more real.

Surprise 5: Sex takes work

"I thought married sex would be automatically amazing." Actually, good sex requires communication, effort, and learning—just like everything else.

Surprise 6: You'll become your parents sometimes

"I swore I'd never nag like my mother. Two months into marriage, I heard her voice coming out of my mouth. My husband does things exactly like his father—things he said he'd never do."

Surprise 7: Little things matter more than big things

"Grand romantic gestures are nice, but daily kindness matters more." Does he make coffee for me? Does she kiss me when she leaves? Those tiny things build or erode intimacy.

Surprise 8: You're building something new

"We both brought expectations from our families of origin. We had to create our own traditions, our own ways of doing things. That was harder but also more meaningful than I expected."

Red Flags In Early Marriage

While adjustment is normal, some patterns signal serious problems:

Seek immediate help if observed:

- Any physical violence or threats
- Verbal abuse, constant criticism, or contempt
- Refusal to communicate or stonewalling
- Addiction emerging or worsening
- Financial deception or secret spending
- Continued emotional attachment to ex-partner
- Refusal to prioritize the marriage
- One partner completely controls the other
- Sexual coercion or ignoring boundaries

These aren't "first year adjustment" issues—these are serious problems requiring professional intervention immediately. Don't wait, hoping things will improve. They won't without help.

What Leads To Success Early In the Marriage?

Here's what helps:

1. Lower Expectations, Increase Grace

Perfect marriages don't exist. Perfect spouses don't exist. You'll both disappoint each other. You'll both be selfish sometimes. Expect this, forgive quickly, and move forward.

2. Over-Communicate

When in doubt, talk about it. Don't assume your spouse knows what you're thinking or feeling. Be explicit about needs, expectations, disappointments, and appreciations.

3. Prioritize Your Relationship

Date nights, daily check-ins, technology-free time together—these aren't luxuries, they're necessities. Your marriage must be protected and nurtured intentionally.

4. Get Help Early

If you're struggling, see a Counsellor during year one, not year five. Early intervention is far more effective than waiting until patterns are entrenched.

5. Remember Why You Married

When frustrated, recall what you love about your spouse. Look at wedding photos. Remember the good times. Don't let current challenges erase the foundation you built.

6. Build Rituals

Create daily, weekly, and annual rituals that are uniquely yours:

• Morning coffee together
• Sunday walks
• Annual anniversary trip
• Holiday traditions

These create continuity and connection amid the chaos of adjustment.

7. Laugh Together

Don't take everything so seriously. Some of your fights will be ridiculous in retrospect. Learn to laugh at yourselves, at the absurdity of learning to share your life, at the inevitable awkwardness of becoming "we" instead of "me."

Realistic Expectations For Year One

By the end of year one, realistic goals are:

• You've established basic household rhythms
• You have a working financial system

• You can have difficult conversations without destroying each other
   • You've weathered at least one significant conflict
   • You understand each other's communication styles better
   • You've set boundaries with families
   • You have some shared rituals and traditions
   • You still like each other and want to continue building together
You don't need to have everything figured out. You don't need perfect harmony. You just need progress, commitment, and willingness to keep working on the relationship.

My First Year

Let me be transparent: Our first year was hard. Really hard. We fought about money—she wanted me to pay for everything, I wanted her to share some of the burden because she was also working. We fought about housework— she expected me to do more domestic tasks than I'd grown up seeing men do. We fought about sex—different desire levels, different expectations. We fought about time together— I felt she spent too much time with her family member and buddies. What saved us:
   • We kept talking, even when conversations were difficult
   • We both committed to figuring it out rather than giving up
   • We gave each other grace for mistakes and misunderstandings
   • We remembered that we were building something new together
   • We laugh at ourselves a lot after the storm is over.
By year two, things were smoother, we had solid patterns and rhythms. But year one? Year one was hard. And that's normal.

Reflection & Assessment

Personal Reflection
   How did I respond when expectations met reality?
   Did I adapt, withdraw, or blame?
Partner Dialogue
   What surprised us most about living together?
   How did we handle disappointment?
Reality Check Tick one:
   ☐ We adapted together
   ☐ We struggled silently

☐ We blamed each other

Looking Forward

If you can survive—and even thrive—through the first year adjustment, you're building skills that will serve you forever:
- Communication under pressure
- Conflict resolution
- Compromise and flexibility
- Boundary setting
- Emotional regulation
- Forgiveness and grace

These aren't just marriage skills; they're life skills.

In the next section, we'll move beyond survival mode to explore how to sustain and strengthen your relationship through the years. We'll discuss the ongoing work of marriage: maintaining intimacy, managing finances wisely, navigating religious differences, staying faithful, and building a partnership that deepens with time.

But first, you have to get through challenges early in the marriage. Be patient with yourself, with your spouse, and with the process. What you're building is worth the difficulty.

Scan this code for a short reflection related to Part II.

PART III - BUILDING AND SUSTAINING: MARRIAGE LIFE

Sustaining marriage requires ongoing investment, and our survey identifies what matters most to couples in both cultures. Family relations play a consistently important role: 52% of African and 39% of American respondents rate family relationships as "very" or "extremely" important to their partnerships. This challenges individualistic models of marriage, suggesting that successful couples maintain strong extended family connections.

Finance reveals complex cross-cultural dynamics. While Americans more often consider money when choosing partners (48% vs 41%), Africans more frequently rate finance as playing a major role in their actual relationships (38% vs 27%). The most telling statistic: 21% of dissatisfied American couples cite financial security as what keeps them together, compared to just 2% in Africa. This suggests American marriages may be more financially entangled—or entrapped—than their African counterparts.

Religion divides the continents most dramatically. Despite similar Christian majorities (77% Africa, 65% USA), Africans integrate faith into relationships at nearly double the rate. Over half of African respondents (54%) say religion plays a "very" or "extremely" important role in their relationships, compared to just 25% of Americans. For cross-cultural couples, this represents a significant potential area of misalignment.

When relationships struggle, respondents identify familiar culprits: unfaithfulness, dishonesty, and irresponsibility top the African list of complaints. American responses, while more varied in expression, echo the same themes. Across cultures, violations of trust and reliability damage relationships more than any other factors.

Pause for Reflection

This part of The Second Bridge is designed to be read as a whole. Before moving to the next section, you are invited to pause and reflect on the ideas explored across all the chapters in this part.

A short reflection questionnaire is available to help you assess insights, patterns, and areas for growth.

Please complete the questionnaire only after reading all chapters in this part. (Scan the code at the end of this section to access the reflection.)

CHAPTER 8: SUSTAINING RELATIONSHIPS

What you do daily determines whether love grows or withers.

Investing in What Matters

You've survived the first year. Congratulations—that's genuinely an achievement. But now comes the real work: sustaining your relationship not just through crisis or adjustment, but through the ordinary days that make up most of life. This chapter explores what keeps marriages alive and thriving—not just surviving—through years and decades. Because while falling in love might be easy, staying in love requires intentional investment.

The Maintenance Myth

Here's a truth that surprises many couples: Relationships don't maintain themselves. They either grow or decay. There is no neutral. Think of your relationship like a garden. You can plant beautiful flowers, but if you stop watering, weeding, and tending them, what happens? The garden doesn't stay the same—it's overtaken by weeds and dies. Your relationship is the same. Without active investment, it deteriorates.

As years go by, partners become like roommates who occasionally had sex. Even when they are not fighting, they stop connecting. They stop dating, stop talking about anything meaningful, stop prioritizing each other. They must actively choose to rebuild what had been eroded.

The Five Investment Categories

Based on my research and experience, sustaining a relationship requires investment in five key areas:

1. Time Investment

This seems obvious, but it's the most commonly neglected investment. Quality time doesn't happen accidentally—you must create it intentionally. Time investment isn't about quantity alone—it's about quality. Sitting on the couch scrolling phones doesn't count as quality time. Neither does discussing logistics about bills and schedules. Quality time means:

• Focused attention on each other
• Meaningful conversation
• Shared experiences that create memories
• Physical affection and intimacy
• Laughter and play

Ask yourself: When was the last time you and your spouse had a conversation that wasn't about logistics? When did you last laugh together? When did you last do something new together? If you can't remember, you're not investing enough time.

2. Emotional Investment

Emotional investment means consistently showing up for your partner emotionally—celebrating their joys, comforting their sorrows, and being present for their daily experiences. Research by Dr. John Gottman shows that successful couples "turn toward" each other's bids for emotional connection rather than turning away or against. A bid might be:

• "Look at this funny video"
• "I had a rough day at work"
• "Did you hear about…….."
• "Want to take a walk?"

Turning toward means engaging: "Let me see! That is funny." "Tell me about it." "No, what happened?" "Yes, let's go."

Turning away means ignoring: continuing to scroll your phone, giving minimal response, changing the subject.

Turning against means rejecting: "I'm busy." "You always complain." "I don't care about that."

Gottman's research found that couples who stayed married turned toward each other's bids 86% of the time. Couples who divorced turned toward only 33% of the time. Emotional investment also means:

• Knowing your partner's inner world (dreams, fears, stresses)
• Expressing appreciation regularly
• Offering comfort during difficult times
• Celebrating victories enthusiastically
• Being curious about their day-to-day life
• Remembering what matters to them

3. Communication Investment

We'll dedicate an entire chapter to communication later, but it deserves mention here as a critical investment area. Sustaining relationships requires:

• Regular check-ins about relationship health
• Discussing problems before they become crises

- Sharing inner thoughts and feelings, not just facts
- Listening actively and empathetically
- Asking meaningful questions
- Creating space for difficult conversations

4. Physical Investment

Physical intimacy—both sexual and non-sexual—requires ongoing investment. Bodies change. Desire fluctuates. Life circumstances affect intimacy. You must adapt and prioritize. Physical investment includes:

- Regular sexual intimacy (frequency varies by couple)
- Non-sexual touch (holding hands, hugging, cuddling)
- Maintaining physical attraction (taking care of your health and appearance)
- Being present during intimacy, not just going through motions
- Adapting to physical changes (aging, illness, childbirth)
- Communicating about desires and needs

5. Growth Investment

Healthy relationships require both partners to keep growing—individually and together. Stagnation kills relationships. Growth investment means:

- Supporting each other's personal development
- Learning new things together
- Having new experiences
- Challenging each other to become better
- Growing spiritually (if religious)
- Developing new skills or hobbies
- Maintaining individual identities while building shared identity

What Erodes Relationships

Understanding what sustains relationships requires understanding what erodes them. Based on my research, here are the primary relationship killers:

Erosion Factor 1: Neglect

Simply not investing. Taking your spouse for granted. Assuming the relationship will be fine without attention. In my case, I poured everything into my career and our kids. I assumed my marriage would always be there. By the time I looked up, my wife and I were strangers and it was over for us.

Erosion Factor 2: Contempt

Contempt—treating your spouse with disrespect, sarcasm, mockery, or disdain—is the single best predictor of divorce according to Gottman's research. Contempt shows up as:

- Eye-rolling
- Mocking
- Name-calling
- Treating your spouse as inferior or stupid
- Expressing disgust
- Hostile humour

I wanted our relation to be based on logic and what made sense all the time. She learned this from me and when I realised the damage this was doing to our relationship and made effort to change my approach, it was too late. She started relating to me on the basis of logic and what made sense which irritated me and led to regular clashes between us.

Erosion Factor 3: Unresolved Resentment

Small hurts, when unaddressed, accumulate into massive resentment. Eventually, resentment poisons everything. For years, she criticized everything I did. How I parented. How I managed money. How I spent my time. I never said anything—I just took it. But inside, I was building this mountain of resentment. One day, I exploded over something minor. She couldn't understand why I was so angry. I couldn't explain that it wasn't about that moment—it was about years of accumulated hurt.

Erosion Factor 4: Comparison

Constantly comparing your spouse to others—to your friend's spouse, to your own idealized fantasy, to who they used to be, to who you wish they were. She kept comparing me to other husbands who were more romantic, more successful, more attentive. She made me feel like I could never measure up. The comparisons created distance because I stopped trying—why compete with an idealized version that doesn't exist?

Erosion Factor 5: External Priorities

When everything else consistently comes before your marriage—work, kids, friends, hobbies, even religious beliefs—the relationship starves. I was a role model to a lot of people, excelling at work, involved in community. Everyone praised me. But my wife felt abandoned. She said, 'You give your best to everyone else except your family.' I didn't see it that way. She was right. I was investing everywhere except where it mattered most.

Erosion Factor 6: Lack of Appreciation

When you stop noticing what your spouse does, stop expressing gratitude, and stop acknowledging their contributions. I felt I was doing so much for the family and never received thank you from my spouse. She didn't notice unless something wasn't done. I felt invisible. That lack of appreciation was discouraging.

Practical Strategies For Sustaining Your Relationship

Based on my experience and survey, here are concrete strategies:
Strategy 1: Daily Connection Rituals
Create small daily practices that keep you connected:
• Morning coffee together before the day starts
• A real kiss (not peck) when leaving and returning
• Evening walks after dinner
• Fifteen minutes of phone-free conversation before bed
• Daily expressions of appreciation
In my current relationship:
1. We eat breakfast together.
2. Give real kiss in the morning wishing each other a great day
3. Spend some time together at the end of the day discussing our day
4. Eat dinner together
5. Pray together where possible
Strategy 2: Weekly Date Time
Protect at least one evening or afternoon per week for focused couple time. This doesn't have to be expensive or elaborate—it just needs to be intentional. Date ideas that work long-term:
• Walks in nature
• Coffee shop conversations
• Cooking new recipes together
• Game nights
• Exploring new parts of your city
• Attending events (concerts, plays, sports)
• Working on projects together
We take walks together for a distance of at least 10 kilometres on Sundays, go on hike, and cinema where possible on weekends. Once in a while, we dine outside in a restaurant of our choice. The key is doing something together where you're engaged with each other, not just side-by-side consuming entertainment.
Strategy 3: Monthly State-of-the-Union
Once a month, have a relationship check-in:

- How are we doing?
- What's working well?
- What needs attention?
- Are there any unresolved issues?
- What do we want to focus on improving?
- How can I be a better partner?

This prevents small issues from becoming big problems and keeps you aligned.

Strategy 4: Annual Relationship Review

Once a year (perhaps on your anniversary), do a deeper review:
- What did we accomplish as a couple this year?
- What challenges did we navigate?
- How have we grown?
- What do we want to achieve next year?
- What patterns need to change?
- What dreams do we still have?

Strategy 5: Surprise and Delight

Long-term relationships need spontaneity and surprise to stay vibrant:
- Unexpected small gifts
- Surprise date plans
- Love notes
- Acts of service your spouse didn't request
- Trying something new together

The keyword is unexpected. Routine is comfortable but can become boring. Inject newness regularly.

Strategy 6: Shared Goals and Projects

Work toward something together:
- Renovating a room
- Training for a race
- Learning a language
- Planning a big trip
- Building a business
- Serving in your community

Shared goals create forward momentum and teamwork.

Strategy 7: Maintain Individual Identity

This seems counterintuitive, but healthy sustained relationships require both partners to maintain individual interests, friendships, and growth. You need to be a whole person to contribute to a healthy partnership.

Strategy 8: Fight Fair and Repair Quickly

Conflict is inevitable. What matters is how you handle it:
• Address issues promptly, don't let resentment build
• Use "I feel" statements rather than accusations
• Listen to understand, not to win
• Apologize sincerely when wrong
• Forgive genuinely when apologized to
• Repair the connection after conflict (hug, hold hands, reconnect)

Strategy 9: Express Appreciation Daily

Make gratitude a daily practice:
• "Thank you for…..."
• "I appreciate that you…..."
• "I noticed you….. and it meant a lot."

Every day, we tell each other one specific thing I appreciate such as "I love you". Not generic 'you're great,' but specific: 'I appreciated that you called to check on me during my stressful meeting' or 'Thank you for making my favourite dinner even though you were tired.' Specificity shows I'm paying attention."

Strategy 10: Protect Your Relationship from External Threats

This means:
• Setting boundaries with work (not bringing work stress home constantly)
• Managing technology (no phones during couple time)
• Balancing kids with marriage (marriage comes first)
• Maintaining appropriate boundaries with opposite-sex friends
• Not allowing family interference
• Limiting social media comparisons

Your relationship needs protection from modern life's countless distractions and demands.

The Seasons Of Marriage

Understanding that relationships have seasons helps maintain perspective. Author Gary Chapman identifies several:

The "Spring" Season: Early marriage, high romance, discovering each other

The "Summer" Season: Building phase—careers, kids, establishing life

The "Fall" Season: Evaluation phase—midlife, reassessing, potential crisis or renewal

The "Winter" Season: Mature love, facing aging, deepening intimacy or drifting apart

Each season requires different investments:
• Spring needs romance and foundation-building

- Summer needs teamwork and stress management
- Fall needs recommitment and adaptation
- Winter needs companionship and care

The couples who thrive are those who recognize their current season and invest appropriately.

When To Seek Help

Even with investment, all relationships face difficult periods. Seek counselling when:
- Communication has broken down completely
- You're considering separation or divorce
- There's been infidelity
- You're stuck in destructive patterns
- You can't resolve conflicts on your own
- One or both of you is deeply unhappy
- Life changes have created distance you can't bridge alone

Couples who sought counselling during difficult periods (not just during crises) had significantly better outcomes. Preventive maintenance through occasional counselling sessions can prevent major breakdowns.

Reflection & Assessment

Personal Reflection

What do I consistently invest in this relationship?

Where have I become complacent or assumed things will take care of themselves?

Partner Dialogue

What makes you feel most valued by me?

Where do you feel I could be more intentional?

Reality Check (1 = Low, 5 = High)

Consistency of effort

Emotional availability

Shared intentional time

The Bottom Line

Sustaining a relationship isn't complicated, but it does require consistency. You don't need grand gestures—you need daily small choices to prioritize your partner and your relationship. Every day, you're making deposits or withdrawals from your relationship account. Small daily deposits—appreciation, attention, affection—compound over time. Small daily withdrawals—neglect, criticism, disconnection—also compound. The question isn't whether you'll face challenges. The question is whether you'll invest enough during good times to carry you through difficult times.

In the next chapters, we'll explore specific areas that require investment: finances, religion, and faithfulness. These areas can either strengthen or destroy your relationship depending on how you handle them. But the foundation is this: Are you actively investing in what matters most?

CHAPTER 9: FINANCE IN MARRIAGE

Money does not destroy relationships — secrecy and misalignment about money do.

Finance plays a nuanced role that differs between continents. While 48% of USA respondents consider finance important in partner selection (vs 41% Africa), African respondents more often cite it as playing a "very" or "extremely" important role in their actual relationships (38% vs 27%). Most tellingly, among USA respondents who would leave their relationships if they could, 21% cite financial security as what prevents them—compared to only 2% in Africa.

Our research reveals a paradox: Americans are more likely to consider finance when choosing partners, yet Africans report money playing a larger role in their daily relationships. This suggests American couples may be more financially interdependent—or more trapped by financial obligations—while African couples find other reasons to stay.

Of those already in relationships, 80% of USA respondents and 75% of African respondents cited it as critical and, four out of the five African couples interviewed said money was important in their relationships. Money isn't just about numbers in bank accounts. Money represents values, priorities, security, power, and freedom. How you handle money reveals what you truly value and whether you trust each other. In my survey that asked: What role does money play in your marriage? A married African male said:

Money plays a vital role. It makes life more comfortable where we can afford to live in safe neighbourhood, get the material things we may need and it enhances our social capital

---

Four out of the five respondents interviewed said money played an important role in their relationship.

Financial strain within African households is rarely only about money. It often carries historical memory—of scarcity, obligation, migration, and fear of failure. When these pressures remain unspoken, they frequently surface as withdrawal, control, or conflict, placing strain on intimacy and trust.

This chapter explores why money matters so much, how to align financially, and how to prevent money from destroying what you've built together.

Why Money Creates Conflict

Before we discuss solutions, let's understand why money generates so much conflict:

Reason 1: Different Money Languages

Just as people have different love languages, people have different money languages shaped by upbringing. For someone who grew up poor, money could mean security and would need savings to feel safe. For a spouse who grew up wealthy, money could mean experiences, and would spend freely because he or she's never worried about not having enough. This fundamental difference in what money means causes constant friction. Common money language differences:
- Spender vs. Saver
- Security-focused vs. Experience-focused
- Generous vs. Frugal
- Impulsive vs. Planner
- Risk-taker vs. Risk-averse

Neither language is wrong, but unrecognized differences create conflict.

Reason 2: Hidden Money Shame

Many people carry shame about money:
- Shame about growing up poor
- Shame about debt
- Shame about spending habits
- Shame about earning less than a spouse

• Shame about financial failures

This shame prevents honest conversation. A man with credit card debt who was too ashamed and did not tell his wife before wedding would make the wife feel betrayed when she discovers —not because of the debt, but because it was not disclosed. The shame could cause more damage than the debt itself.

Reason 3: Power Dynamics

Money often represents power in relationships:
• Who earns more may feel entitled to more say
• Who manages money may control access
• Financial dependence creates vulnerability
• Different contributions can create resentment

Imagine a woman who stopped working to raise children. Suddenly, she has to ask her husband for money for everything. He might not be controlling, but she felt powerless. You have to discuss how to maintain equality when one party is not contributing financially.

Reason 4: Different Financial Goals

Conflict arises when partners have incompatible financial priorities:
• Paying off debt vs. investing
• Saving for retirement vs. enjoying life now
• Supporting extended family vs. building own wealth
• Private schools for kids vs. saving for college
• Expensive home vs. simple living

These aren't just financial decisions—they're life philosophy differences.

Reason 5: External Financial Pressure

Money conflicts intensify under external pressure:
• Job loss or income reduction
• Unexpected expenses (medical, car, home repair)
• Economic downturns
• Family financial emergencies
• Debt accumulation

Stress makes us less patient, less generous, and more reactive—perfect conditions for money fights.

Essential Financial Conversations

Before marriage and regularly throughout, couples must discuss:

Conversation 1: Current Financial Reality

Full disclosure of:

- Income and earning potential
- Existing debt (student loans, credit cards, medical, personal)
- Credit scores
- Assets (savings, investments, property)
- Financial obligations (child support, family support, etc.)
- Spending habits and money history

Conversation 2: Money Values and History

Discuss:

- How money was handled in your family growing up
- What money means to you (security? freedom? status?)
- Your biggest money fears
- Your money dreams and goals
- Spending vs. saving orientation
- Views on debt
- Generosity and charitable giving

Understanding each other's money story creates empathy for current behaviours.

Conversation 3: Financial Management System

Decide together:

- Joint accounts, separate accounts, or hybrid?
- Who pays which bills?
- Who manages the day-to-day finances?
- What spending limit requires discussion?
- How will you make major financial decisions?
- How often will you review finances together?

Conversation 4: Financial Goals

Align on:

- Emergency fund target
- Debt payoff plan
- Retirement savings goals
- Home ownership plans
- Children's education savings
- Major purchases timeline
- Dream vacation or experience goals

Write these down. Review them regularly. Adjust as circumstances change.

Conversation 5: Extended Family Financial Obligations

Especially critical for cross-cultural couples:

- What obligations exist to parents, siblings, extended family?
- How much is reasonable to give/lend?
- Under what circumstances?

> • How will you make these decisions?

Set clear boundaries before facing requests.

Practical Financial Strategies

Here are strategies that work:

Strategy 1: Regular Money Meetings

Schedule weekly or monthly financial check-ins:

- Review income and expenses
- Discuss upcoming bills and purchases
- Address any concerns
- Celebrate progress toward goals
- Adjust budget as needed

Make these meetings neutral, not accusatory. You're teammates solving problems together, not adversaries fighting over resources.

Strategy 2: The Budget That Works for You

There's no one right budgeting system. Find what works for your unique situation: Zero-based budgeting: Every amount spent has an assigned purpose 50/30/20 rule: 50% needs, 30% wants, 20% savings/debt

Envelope system: Cash allocated to categories Percentage-based, income divided by percentages to different purposes

What matters isn't which system you use but that you have one and both follow it.

Strategy 3: Automatic Savings and Bill Pay

Automate what you can:

- Savings transferred to separate account at paycheck
- Bills paid automatically
- Retirement contributions deducted pre-paycheck

Automation removes daily decision-making and ensures priorities are funded first.

Strategy 4: The "Fun Money" Allowance

Each partner gets equal amount of discretionary money to spend without explanation or judgment. This preserves individual autonomy within the larger shared financial plan. The amount doesn't matter, what matters is equality and freedom.

Strategy 5: Emergency Fund First

Before aggressive debt payoff or investing, build 3-6 months of expenses in an emergency fund. This buffer prevents financial stress from destroying your relationship when unexpected expenses arise.

Strategy 6: Debt Elimination Plan

If you have debt, create and follow a clear plan:
• List all debts (amount, interest rate, minimum payment)
• Choose strategy (debt snowball or debt avalanche)
• Set timeline and milestones
• Celebrate progress

Pay off debt together as a team, not blaming whoever brought it into the marriage.

Strategy 7: No Financial Secrets

Agree to complete transparency:
• No hidden accounts
• No secret spending
• No concealed debt
• No major purchases without discussion

Financial infidelity destroys trust as completely as sexual infidelity.

Strategy 8: Unified Front on Extended Family

If one partner's family makes financial requests, discuss together before responding. Present a unified decision.

Strategy 9: Annual Financial Review

Once per year, do a comprehensive review:
• Net worth calculation
• Progress toward goals
• Insurance needs
• Estate planning updates
• Tax strategy
• Investment allocation
• Major upcoming expenses

Consider working with a financial planner for this annual review.

Strategy 10: Celebrate Financial Wins

When you pay off debt, reach a savings goal, or achieve a financial milestone, celebrate together. This positive reinforcement keeps you motivated and bonds you through shared achievement.

Navigating Specific Financial Challenges

Challenge 1: Income Disparity

When one partner earns significantly more:
Avoid:
• The higher earner making all decisions
• The lower earner feeling inferior or powerless
• Resentment building on either side
Instead:

• Treat all income as "ours" not "mine"
• Make decisions jointly regardless of earning ratio
• Value non-financial contributions equally
• Consider percentage-based contributions if keeping some separate finances

Challenge 2: Stay-at-Home Parent

When one partner leaves workforce:

Address:

• How will non-earning spouse access money without asking permission?
• How will you ensure equality despite financial dependence?
• What happens to career/earning potential long-term?
• How will retirement savings be maintained?

One solution: The stay-at-home parent has equal access to all accounts and an equal personal spending allowance. Their contribution through childcare and household management is valued in family discussions.

Challenge 3: Job Loss

When income suddenly drops:

Immediate steps:

• Review and cut non-essential expenses
• Access emergency fund
• Communicate clearly about stress and fears
• Support each other emotionally through the transition
• Don't blame or shame

The couples who survive financial crisis without relationship damage are those who treat it as a shared problem to solve together, not a failure of one partner.

Challenge 4: Unexpected Major Expense

Medical emergency, car crash, home repair, legal issue:

Response:

• Use emergency fund (this is why you built it)
• Adjust budget to accommodate
• Explore payment plans or assistance
• Don't make it bigger by also fighting about it
• Work together to recover financially

Challenge 5: Different Financial Risk Tolerance

One partner wants to invest aggressively; the other wants safety:

Compromise:

• Allocate portfolio with both strategies
• Each partner manages portion according to their preference

• Set boundaries on maximum risk exposure
• Review and adjust regularly

The key is finding middle ground rather than one partner dominating or being dismissed.

Warning Signs Of Financial Trouble

Seek help immediately if you notice:
• Hiding spending or debt
• Fighting constantly about money
• One partner controlling all finances without transparency
• Accumulating debt despite adequate income
• Unable to discuss money without explosive conflict
• Financial stress causing health problems
• Avoiding bills or financial reality

Financial counselling—whether through a financial planner, credit Counsellor, or therapist specializing in money issues—can prevent financial problems from destroying your marriage.

The Bigger Picture

Money conflicts are rarely actually about money. They're about:
• Trust (Can I trust you with our financial future?)
• Respect (Do you respect my financial concerns and values?)
• Security (Will we be okay financially?)
• Partnership (Are we working together or against each other?)
• Values (What matters most to us?)

When you fight about money, ask yourself: "What am I really upset about?" Often, addressing the underlying emotional issue helps resolve the surface financial conflict.

Reflection & Assessment

Personal Reflection
What fears or beliefs about money do I carry into this relationship?
How does money affect my sense of power, security, or control?

Partner Dialogue
What does money represent to you emotionally?
Where do our financial values align or clash?

Reality Check Tick all that apply:

☐ We are transparent about finances
☐ We avoid financial conversations
☐ We share financial goals

Final Thoughts On Finances

Money will either unite you as you work toward shared goals, or divide you as you fight over scarce resources. The choice is largely yours. Financial alignment doesn't require identical views on money. It requires:

- Honest communication
- Shared goals
- Mutual respect
- Fair system that both can live with
- Regular review and adjustment
- Commitment to solving problems together

Invest the time to get your finances aligned. The payoff—reduced stress, increased trust, achieved goals—is worth every difficult conversation.

In the next chapter, we'll explore another area that requires alignment: religion and spirituality in marriage.

CHAPTER 10: RELIGION IN MARRIAGE

*When values collide, affection alone cannot hold the
marriage together.*

Religion reveals the survey's most dramatic cultural divide. Despite Christianity being dominant in both samples (77% Africa, 65% USA), attitudes toward religion's role in relationships differ dramatically:

61% of Africans vs 36% of Americans consider religion important in partner selection

54% of Africans vs 25% of Americans say religion plays a "very/extremely important" role

51% of Americans rate religion as "not so" or "not at all" important—double the African rate.

---

*Our data reveals that religious identification doesn't
predict religious importance in relationships. While both
continents show Christian majorities, African respondents
integrate faith into their relationship decisions at nearly
twice the rate of Americans. This suggests that religiosity
in relationships reflects cultural context as much as
personal belief.*

The Power Of Shared Faith

When asked the question *"What did you consider in choosing your partner?"* two of the five African respondents interviewed said *"Religion and Religious Background"* and another said *"He is God-fearing."* When asked the question "What role does religion play in your relationship currently?" all five African respondents said religion plays an important role. Some of the comments included:

*Religion is fundamental, praying together and sharing the word of God bonds us more as a married couple.",
"Religion plays its own role by helping us maintain balance. Religion (faith) is central to our manage.",
Religion is the most important thing in our relationship as we need to pass on the right faith to our children.", and
"Religion gives us values to emulate and we constantly look and review our acts towards fellow man....*

For couples who share religious beliefs and practice, faith can be a tremendous blessing in many ways including:

Shared Value System

Religion gives marriage a common foundation. When partners disagree about something, they could go to religious books of their common faith together and find guidance which becomes a reference point outside ourselves. Shared faith provides:
- Common moral framework
- Shared vocabulary for discussing values
- External authority both respect
- Community support through church/mosque/temple
- Rituals that bond you (prayer, worship, religious holidays)

Purpose Beyond Yourselves

Faith reminds couples that marriage isn't just about happiness, but about serving God, serving each other, and serving the community. This bigger purpose carries the marriage through times when partners don't feel 'in love.'

Tools for Conflict Resolution

Religious faith often provides specific guidance for handling marriage conflicts:
- Forgiveness practices
- Humility and admitting wrong
- Seeking Counsel from spiritual leaders
- Prayer for wisdom and patience
- Religious texts offering relationship guidance

Community Support

Religious communities often provide:
- Marriage enrichment programs

- Counselling from pastoral staff
- Mentoring from older couples
- Social support during crises
- Accountability for marital health

However, this support only helps if the community is healthy. Toxic religious communities can damage marriages.

The Challenges Of Shared Faith

Even when couples share faith, challenges arise:

Challenge 1: Different Levels of Devotion

One partner is deeply devout; the other is casual in practice. One partner might want to attend every religious activity whilst the other might want to do some other activities. This intensity difference creates tension around:

- Time spent in religious activities
- Financial giving to religious institutions
- Social life centered on religious community
- Parenting approaches
- How faith is expressed

Challenge 2: Religious Control

When one partner uses religion to control, manipulate, or justify bad behaviour. Warning signs:

- Using religious teachings to demand submission or obedience
- Claiming God told them something to win an argument
- Using religion to prohibit reasonable activities or relationships
- Spiritual abuse (using faith to induce guilt or shame)
- Isolating partner from non-religious friends or family

True faith strengthens both partners. It doesn't tear one down to elevate the other.

Challenge 3: Religious Community Interference

When religious leaders or community members interfere inappropriately in marriage. Examples:

- Spiritual leaders taking sides in marital conflicts
- Religious community pressuring couple to stay in unhealthy marriage
- Congregation members gossiping about marital problems
- Religious authority undermining professional counselling
- Community imposing rigid expectations on marriage roles

Challenge 4: Faith Crisis

When one partner experiences doubt, faith transition, or deconversion: One partner feeling betrayed when the other lost faith when the relationship is built around religious community, values, parenting, and everything. Faith changes can threaten marriages because:

* Shared foundation shifts
* Community may pressure the faithful spouse to leave
* Children's spiritual upbringing becomes contested
* Social life changes
* Values may diverge

Challenge 5: Religious Rigidity

When religious rules become more important than the relationship it could interfere in the functioning of the with relationship.

The Interfaith Marriage Challenge

Couples from different religious traditions face unique complications: Interfaith challenges include:

Religious Practice Conflicts

* Whose religious holidays are celebrated?
* Where do you worship?
* How do you pray together?
* What dietary restrictions are followed?
* What religious obligations take precedence?

Family and Community Pressure

Both families may:

* Disapprove of the marriage
* Pressure for conversion
* Exclude the 'outsider' spouse
* Refuse to participate in religious ceremonies
* Create loyalty tests

Children's Religious Identity

The most contentious interfaith question: How do we raise our children? Options couples choose:

* Raise children in one faith (often the more devout parent's)
* Expose children to both faiths and let them choose as adults
* Raise children with no specific faith
* Alternate years or children between faiths
* Create hybrid practice incorporating both traditions

Each approach has implications:

One Faith Approach: Clear but may alienate other partner or their family

Both Faiths Approach: Inclusive but can confuse children or satisfy neither tradition

No Faith Approach: Neutral but may disappoint both families and leave children without spiritual foundation

Hybrid Approach: Creative but may not be accepted by either religious community

Practical Guidance For Navigating Religious Differences

Whether you're same-faith with different intensity, or interfaith, these strategies help:

Strategy 1: Deep Conversation Before Marriage

Discuss explicitly:

- What do you believe and why?
- How important is faith to your identity?
- What religious practices are non-negotiable?
- What practices are you flexible about?
- How will we handle religious holidays?
- What role will religion play in our home?
- How will we raise children spiritually?
- What if one of us changes faith or loses faith?
- Can we attend each other's religious services?
- What boundaries exist with families around religion?

Have these conversations early, repeatedly, and honestly. Don't assume you'll "figure it out later."

Strategy 2: Respect Without Conversion Pressure

For interfaith couples, agree:

- Neither will pressure the other to convert
- Both will respect each other's faith
- Neither will mock or demean the other's beliefs
- Both will support each other's religious practice
- Conversion, if it occurs, will be voluntary and unpressured

That agreement removed enormous tension.

Strategy 3: Find Common Ground

Most religions share core values:

- Love and compassion
- Honesty and integrity
- Service to others
- Family commitment
- Justice and fairness

Focus on shared values rather than doctrinal differences.

Strategy 4: Create Shared Rituals

Even if you can't share religious practice fully, create spiritual rituals you can do together:
- Gratitude practice before meals
- Meditation or reflection time
- Service projects in your community
- Nature walks as spiritual practice
- Reading spiritual texts together and discussing
- Praying in your own traditions, but at the same time

Strategy 5: Establish Boundaries with Religious Communities

Protect your marriage from religious community interference:
- Our marriage decisions are ours to make
- We won't tolerate family pressure to divorce
- Religious leaders are advisors, not decision-makers
- We'll leave religious communities that harm our marriage
- We present a united front to religious authorities

Strategy 6: Get Premarital Counselling from Someone Trained in Interfaith Issues

If you're interfaith, find a Counsellor experienced in navigating religious differences. Many religious Counsellors are biased toward conversion or will refuse to counsel interfaith couples. Seek someone who respects both traditions and can help you create workable solutions.

Strategy 7: Plan for Children Early

Don't wait until you're pregnant to discuss how you'll raise children spiritually. Decide beforehand:
- What faith tradition(s) will we teach?
- What religious ceremonies will we perform?
- Where will we attend services?
- How will we handle religious education?
- What if we disagree later?

Write down your agreement and revisit it periodically.

Strategy 8: Be Prepared to Disappoint Families

Interfaith couples often cannot please both sets of parents. Accept this reality and prioritize your marriage over family approval.

When Religious Differences Become Deal breakers

Sometimes, religious differences are genuinely incompatible. Consider ending the relationship if:
- One partner demands conversion, and the other refuses

• Religious requirements make daily life impossible (extreme dietary restrictions, conflicting worship schedules, etc.)

• Families' religious pressure is destroying the relationship

• You cannot agree on how to raise children

• One partner's religious practice involves beliefs or behaviours the other finds morally repugnant

• The stress of religious difference is making both miserable

Better to acknowledge incompatibility before marriage than divorce after.

The Role Of Faith In My Own Marriage

Let me share personally: Faith has been foundational in my marriage. Our shared practice of prayer, worship, and religious principles gives us a common language and values. When we disagree, we can appeal to shared authority. When we're hurting, we have spiritual resources to draw on.

However, I've watched interfaith friends build beautiful marriages through mutual respect, clear agreements, and a focus on shared values. It's harder, but it's possible when both partners are committed.

Reflection & Assessment

Personal Reflection

How central is faith or belief to my identity?

Do I expect my partner to believe or practise as I do?

Partner Dialogue

How do we honour belief differences or similarities?

Where does faith unite or divide us?

Reality Check (1–5)

Mutual respect for beliefs

Shared spiritual practices

The Bottom Line

Religion can be a tremendous asset to marriage when:

• Beliefs are genuinely shared or respected

• Faith communities are healthy and supportive

• Religious practice brings couples together rather than drives them apart

• Neither partner uses religion to control or manipulate

- Both partners grow spiritually in ways that strengthen the relationship

Religion becomes a liability when:

- Differences are unacknowledged or minimized
- One partner uses faith as a weapon
- Religious communities interfere destructively
- Beliefs change and couples can't adapt
- Neither partner is willing to compromise

Whatever your religious situation, approach it with honesty, respect, and willingness to work through differences. Your spiritual life affects every aspect of your marriage—handle it with the seriousness it deserves.

CHAPTER 11: FAITHFULNESS AND INTIMACY

Faithfulness is not merely physical loyalty; it is emotional and psychological alignment.

The Foundation of Trust

Let's discuss the most sensitive topic in marriage: faithfulness and intimacy. This chapter explores what faithfulness truly means, how to maintain intimacy through years and decades, and how to navigate one of the most common challenges marriages face.

What Breaks Relationships

When asked what they don't like about their relationships, African respondents provide clear answers: Unfaithfulness (8%), Lying (4%), Irresponsibility (5%), and Alcoholism (2%). The USA responses, while more varied, echo themes of dishonesty, emotional unavailability, and addiction.

Defining Faithfulness

Faithfulness seems straightforward—don't have sex with anyone else, right? But some people might consider the following unfaithful:
- Sexual intercourse with someone else
- Oral sex with someone else
- Romantic dating/relationship with someone else
- Emotional affair (deep emotional intimacy with someone else)
- Kissing someone else romantically
- Sexting or explicit messages with someone else
- Using pornography regularly
- Strip club attendance
- Close friendships with opposite sex
- Flirting with others
- Following/liking provocative social media accounts
- Occasional pornography use

Couples must define faithfulness explicitly for their relationship. What one person considers harmless, another considers betrayal.

Physical Faithfulness

Let's start with the obvious: Sexual exclusivity is foundational to most marriages.

Why does sexual infidelity hurt so profoundly?

It's not just about the physical act. Sexual infidelity breaks:
- Trust (the foundation of everything)
- Safety (you no longer feel secure)
- Commitment (promises were broken)
- Respect (your worth was disregarded)
- Intimacy (the unique bond between you is violated)

Preventing Physical Infidelity

Based on couples who maintained faithfulness through decades:

Prevention Strategy 1: Maintain Strong Primary Relationship

Infidelity rarely happens in satisfied, connected marriages. It happens when:
- Intimacy has decreased or disappeared
- Emotional connection has eroded
- Conflict is constant
- One or both partners feel unappreciated
- Sexual needs are unmet
- Communication has broken down

The best prevention for infidelity is a healthy marriage. Invest in your relationship—it's your best protection.

Prevention Strategy 2: Set Clear Boundaries

Decide together:
- What opposite-sex friendships look like
- What one-on-one time with the opposite sex is acceptable
- What information you share with opposite-sex friends
- How you handle attraction to others (because attraction will happen)
- What you do when someone flirts with you

One couple's boundaries:
- No one-on-one meals or drinks with opposite sex unless spouse knows
- No private conversations about marital problems with opposite sex
- No physical affection beyond professional/casual greeting
- If attraction develops, tell your spouse immediately and distance yourself from that person

* Regular check-ins about whether these boundaries need adjustment

Prevention Strategy 3: Avoid High-Risk Situations

Infidelity rarely "just happens." It develops through progressive boundary violations:

* Innocent friendship
* Increased communication
* Sharing personal information
* Emotional intimacy
* Physical touch
* Sexual activity

Prevent this progression by:

* Limiting private time with potential affair partners
* Not sharing marital problems with opposite-sex friends
* Avoiding alcohol-fuelled situations with temptation
* Eliminating secrecy (if you'd hide it from your spouse, don't do it)
* Recognizing attraction early and creating distance

Prevention Strategy 4: Prioritize Sexual Intimacy

Sexual satisfaction doesn't guarantee faithfulness, but sexual neglect creates vulnerability. When one partner's sexual needs are consistently unmet, temptation increases.

This doesn't justify infidelity—it never does. But it's reality: maintaining satisfying sexual intimacy is protective.

Prevention Strategy 5: Stay Connected During High-Risk Periods

Certain life stages increase infidelity risk:

* After childbirth (especially when sexual intimacy decreases)
* During career stress or success
* When traveling for work
* During midlife transitions
* When one partner is ill or unavailable
* After major life disappointments

During these periods, intentionally increase connection rather than letting distance grow.

Emotional Faithfulness

Emotional affairs—deep emotional intimacy with someone other than your spouse—can be as damaging as physical affairs, sometimes more so.

Signs of Emotional Affair:
• Sharing intimate thoughts/feelings with someone else rather than spouse
    • Thinking about the other person constantly
    • Comparing spouse unfavourably to the other person
    • Hiding the relationship or minimizing its significance
    • Seeking emotional support from them rather than spouse
    • Prioritizing time with them over spouse
    • Feeling guilty about the relationship
    • Defensive when spouse asks about it

How Emotional Affairs Start:
Usually innocently:
    • Co-worker providing support during a stressful time
    • Friend listening sympathetically to marital problems
    • Online connection offering understanding
    • Old flame reconnecting on social media

The shift from friendship to an emotional affair happens when:
• You start sharing things you're not sharing with your spouse
• You seek this person's approval or validation
• You feel excitement or anticipation about interacting with them
• You hide or minimize the relationship to your spouse
• Your emotional energy goes to them rather than your spouse

Prevention:
Same boundaries that prevent physical affairs prevent emotional ones:
    • Share marital problems with spouse or Counsellor, not opposite-sex friends
    • Maintain transparency about friendships
    • Recognize emotional intimacy developing and create distance
    • Invest emotional energy in your marriage, not outside relationships
    • If you find yourself attracted, tell spouse and increase marital connection

Rebuilding After Infidelity

What if faithfulness has already been broken? Can marriages survive infidelity?

Recovery is possible, but it requires:

1. Complete End to the Affair
The unfaithful partner must:

- End all contact with the affair partner immediately
- Be completely transparent about the affair
- Accept full responsibility without excuses
- Express genuine remorse (not just regret at being caught)
- Understand the depth of hurt caused

If the unfaithful partner minimizes, blames the betrayed partner, or maintains contact with the affair partner, recovery is impossible.

2. Complete Transparency

The unfaithful partner must:

- Provide access to all communications (phone, email, social media)
- Account for time and whereabouts
- Answer all questions honestly, even painful ones
- Accept loss of privacy as a consequence of broken trust
- Maintain this transparency until trust is rebuilt (months or years)

3. Professional Help

Very few couples recover from infidelity without counselling. Find a therapist experienced in infidelity recovery who can:

- Help the unfaithful partner understand why it happened
- Help the betrayed partner process trauma and decide whether to stay
- Guide both through rebuilding trust
- Address underlying marital issues that created vulnerability
- Develop a relapse prevention plan

4. Time and Patience

Trust isn't rebuilt quickly. Expect:

- Intense emotions (rage, grief, fear) for months
- Triggers and setbacks
- Questions repeating as the betrayed partner processes
- Need for reassurance repeatedly
- Gradual healing over 1-3 years minimum

The unfaithful partner must accept that recovery takes as long as it takes. Rushing or pressuring the betrayed partner to "get over it" prevents healing.

5. Addressing Root Issues

Infidelity is a symptom, not the disease. Recovery requires addressing:

- What was broken in the marriage beforehand?
- What needs weren't being met?
- What attracted the unfaithful partner to the affair partner?
- What boundaries were insufficient?

• What changes must happen to prevent recurrence?

This doesn't excuse infidelity—the unfaithful partner is responsible for their choice regardless of marital problems. But understanding context helps prevent recurrence.

When Recovery Isn't Possible:

Some situations make recovery unlikely:

• Unrepentant unfaithful partner
• Multiple affairs
• Ongoing lies after discovery
• Refusal to the end affair
• No remorse, only regret at consequences
• Unwillingness to do recovery work
• Continued betrayals during recovery attempt

In these cases, divorce may be healthier than staying in a marriage where trust cannot be rebuilt.

Maintaining Sexual Intimacy

Now let's discuss maintaining satisfying sexual intimacy through years of marriage—the positive side of faithfulness.

Why Sexual Intimacy Matters:

Sex isn't everything in marriage, but it's not nothing. Sexual intimacy:

• Creates unique bonding
• Releases stress
• Demonstrates desire and attraction
• Meets important physical and emotional needs
• Differentiates marriage from other relationships

Common Sexual Challenges:

Challenge 1: Desire Discrepancy

One partner wants sex more frequently than the other.
Solutions:

• Discuss ideal frequency and find a compromise
• Schedule sex (yes, it can still be romantic)
• Address why desire is low (medical issues? stress? past trauma?)
• Increase non-sexual affection
• Vary types of sexual activity
• Consider that desire is responsive for many people (it increases through engagement rather than preceding it)

Challenge 2: Physical Changes

Bodies change through:

- Aging
- Pregnancy and childbirth
- Illness or injury
- Menopause
- Medication side effects
- Weight changes

These changes affect sexual function and confidence.

Solutions:

- Communicate openly about physical changes and concerns
- Adapt sexual activities as bodies change
- Seek medical help for physical issues (pain, dysfunction, low libido)
- Reassure partner of continued attraction
- Remember sex isn't just about perfect bodies—it's about connection

Challenge 3: Stress and Exhaustion

The primary killer of sexual intimacy: too tired, too stressed, too busy.

Solutions:

- Morning sex (when you're rested)
- Schedule sex dates
- Reduce activities and commitments
- Share household labour more equally
- Recognize that "too tired for sex" often means "too tired for everything"—address the overwhelm
- Remember that sex can relieve stress, not just add to it

Challenge 4: Boredom or Routine

Sex becomes predictable and loses excitement.

Solutions:

- Try new things (positions, locations, times)
- Communicate fantasies and desires
- Read books about sexuality together
- Flirt and build anticipation
- Date each other again
- Remember that novelty doesn't require extreme activities—small changes refresh

Challenge 5: Past Sexual Trauma

Unresolved sexual abuse or assault affects current intimacy. If past trauma interferes with current intimacy:

- Seek therapy specialized in trauma
- Communicate needs and boundaries to spouse

- Be patient with the healing process
- Understand that triggers and setbacks are normal
- Remember that healing is possible with proper support

Strategies for Maintaining Sexual Intimacy:

Strategy 1: Talk About Sex

Most couples don't discuss sex explicitly. They assume, hope, or hint. This doesn't work.

Talk about:
- What you enjoy
- What you want to try
- What doesn't work for you
- Your ideal frequency
- When you feel most desirable
- What builds or kills desire for you

Strategy 2: Prioritize Non-Sexual Affection

Many couples only touch sexually or not at all. This creates pressure.

Increase:
- Holding hands
- Hugging
- Kissing (real kisses, not pecks)
- Cuddling
- Massage
- Casual touches throughout the day

Non-sexual affection builds connection and makes sexual touch more natural.

Strategy 3: Date Your Spouse

Romance doesn't end with marriage. Keep courting:
- Regular dates
- Flirting
- Compliments
- Surprises
- Anticipation-building

Strategy 4: Address Medical Issues

Don't suffer through:
- Pain during sex
- Erectile dysfunction
- Low libido
- Vaginal dryness

- Hormonal issues

See doctors. Use medications or treatments. Sexual function is health—take it seriously.

Strategy 5: Make Sex a Priority

If you wait until you're not tired and have free time, you'll never have sex. Intentionally prioritize it:

- Schedule it if necessary
- Protect your bedroom from intrusions (lock the door)
- Create an atmosphere conducive to intimacy
- Treat it as important as other commitments

The Pornography Question

This is increasingly relevant and increasingly divisive:

Why Pornography Creates Problems:

- Creates unrealistic expectations
- Replaces actual intimacy with virtual
- Can become compulsive
- Often kept secret (violation of trust)
- Partner feels inadequate or replaced
- Changes how the user views sex and partner

Addressing Pornography:

If it's creating problems:

- Discuss honestly without shame
- Decide together what's acceptable in your marriage
- If use is compulsive, seek help
- Increase actual intimacy
- Address underlying issues (dissatisfaction, stress, escapism)

Personal Reflection

What does faithfulness mean to me beyond physical loyalty?

Do I create emotional safety in this relationship?

Partner Dialogue

What helps you feel emotionally close?

What behaviours damage trust for you?

Reality Check (1–5)

☐ Emotional intimacy is strong

☐ Physical intimacy is strong

☐ Trust needs rebuilding

The Bottom Line

Faithfulness and intimacy aren't just about avoiding bad behaviours. They're about actively building something good:
• Deep trust
• Satisfying connection
• Physical and emotional intimacy
• Exclusive bond
This requires:
• Clear boundaries
• Open communication
• Consistent investment
• Adaptation through life changes
• Willingness to work through challenges
Your sexual and emotional intimacy is worth protecting and nurturing. It's the private sanctuary of your marriage—guard it carefully and tend it lovingly.

Scan this code for a short reflection related to Part III.

PART IV - FAMILY DYNAMICS: CHILDREN AND CHOICES

Children fundamentally reshape relationship dynamics, serving as both the greatest joy and the strongest chain. Among respondents who would consider leaving their relationships, children emerge as the primary reason to stay: 51% in Africa and 35% in USA. No other factor comes close. Single parenthood presents measurable challenges to new relationships.

Our data shows single parents trust their partners at rates 10-12 percentage points lower than non-single parents—a pattern consistent across both continents (81% vs 91% in Africa; 83% vs 95% in USA). This trust deficit, likely born of past relationship trauma, creates an additional hurdle for single parents seeking lasting love.

The survey includes 25% single parents in Africa and 18% in USA, providing substantial insight into this demographic. Their experiences suggest that while single parenthood complicates new relationships, it doesn't preclude happiness—many report satisfaction rates comparable to the general population once trust is established.

Pause for Reflection

This part of *The Second Bridge* is designed to be read as a whole. Before moving to the next section, you are invited to pause and reflect on the ideas explored across all the chapters in this part.

A short reflection questionnaire is available to help you assess insights, patterns, and areas for growth.

Please complete the questionnaire only after reading all chapters in this part. (Scan the code at the end of this section to access the reflection.)

CHAPTER 12: CHILDREN IN MARRIAGE

*Children strengthen a healthy marriage and expose a fragile
one.*

Joy, Challenge, and Choice
Few topics in marriage carry as much weight as children. Whether
to have them, when to have them, how many to have, how to raise
them—and what happens when plans don't unfold as expected. This
chapter explores the full spectrum of experiences around children in
marriage. Perhaps no finding is more striking than children's role in
maintaining relationships. Among those who would otherwise leave
their relationships:

Africa: 51% cite children as what prevents them from leaving
USA: 35% cite children

Children change the calculus of commitment. Our survey
found that among respondents who would consider leaving their
relationships, over half of African respondents and over a third of
Americans cite children as the primary reason they stay. This isn't
necessarily unhealthy—it may reflect mature recognition that children's
needs sometimes outweigh personal dissatisfaction. But it raises
important questions about what we owe ourselves versus what we owe
our children.

THE CHILDREN QUESTION

Cultural differences emerged:
In many African societies, childlessness carries a significant stigma,
and children represent security, legacy, and social status. In some other
cultures, children are increasingly viewed as one option among many
for a fulfilling life.

Neither perspective is inherently right or wrong, but cross-cultural
couples must navigate these differences explicitly.

Planning For Children
The most successful couples discuss children thoroughly before
marriage:

Essential Pre-Marriage Questions:
1. Do we both want children?
2. If yes, how many?
3. When do we want to start trying?
4. What if we face infertility?
5. Are we open to adoption or fertility treatments?
6. How will we share parenting responsibilities?
7. What parenting style will we use?
8. How will we handle discipline?
9. What values do we want to instil?
10. How will we balance parenting with our marriage?
11. Will one parent stay home, or will both work?
12. How will children affect our finances?
13. Where do we want to raise children?
14. What role will extended family play?
15. How will we handle disagreements about parenting?
Discuss explicitly and honestly before committing.

The Reality Of Parenting

Let me be blunt: Parenting is harder than anyone tells you.
The Challenging aspect includes:
- Less time together as a couple
- Decreased sexual frequency and intimacy
- Financial stress
- Sleep deprivation (especially early years)
- Disagreements about parenting approaches
- Loss of spontaneity and freedom
- Feeling overwhelmed

The First Child: Marriage Earthquake
Why is the transition so hard?
Reason 1: Sleep Deprivation
Nothing prepared most couples for the sustained sleep deprivation of new parenthood. Sleep deprivation causes:
- Irritability and short tempers
- Decreased cognitive function
- Emotional volatility
- Depression and anxiety
- Physical exhaustion

Reason 2: Identity Shift

You're not just spouses anymore—you're parents. This shift is profound:

- Your entire schedule revolves around a baby
- Your body changes (especially for mothers)
- Your priorities shift
- Your relationship becomes functional rather than romantic
- Your freedom disappears

Reason 3: Division of Labour Conflicts

Even couples who intended equality often fell into traditional patterns:

- Mothers did more childcare even when both parents worked
- Fathers felt excluded from parenting or relegated to "helper" status
- Resentment built up about unequal loads
- Unspoken expectations caused conflict

In African culture, childcare is "women's work." But a wife who works full-time expects some help with—changing diapers, feeding, and night wake-ups. Most African men are not raised to do these things, and this could create tension if expectations are not aligned.

Reason 4: Sexual Intimacy Decline

Physical recovery from childbirth, hormonal changes, exhaustion, and body image issues affect intimacy:

- Many women need 6-12 weeks (or longer) for physical recovery
- Breastfeeding affects hormones and desire
- Exhaustion leaves no energy for sex
- Body changes affect confidence
- Fear of another pregnancy

Some men resent the baby sometimes because the wife has no physical or emotional energy left for them. The men feel replaced which requires an honest conversation about maintaining the marriage amid parenthood.

Navigating the Transition:

Strategy 1: Adjust Expectations

The first year of parenthood is survival mode. Lower expectations for:

- House cleanliness
- Career productivity
- Social life
- Elaborate meals
- Marital harmony

Just survive. It gets easier.

Strategy 2: Divide Labour Explicitly

Don't assume. Discuss and divide:
- Night wake-ups
- Diaper changes
- Feeding
- Household chores
- Errands
- Baby's schedule management

Write it down if needed. Renegotiate as circumstances change.

Strategy 3: Protect Your Marriage

Amid baby care:
- Talk about something other than the baby
- Touch each other non-sexually
- Thank each other for specific things
- Tag-team so each gets breaks
- Remember you are partners, not just co-parents

Setting aside some time after the baby's bedtime to connect with no phones, no TV, just talking could help and even when you are too tired to talk, spend some time together in silence.

Strategy 4: Ask for and Accept Help

Accept help with:
- Meal preparation
- House cleaning
- Baby holding so you can shower or nap
- Errands

Pride prevents many couples from accepting the needed help. Survival requires swallowing pride.

Strategy 5: Address Postpartum Mental Health

Postpartum depression and anxiety affect some mothers and a significant percentage of fathers. Symptoms include:
- Persistent sadness or emptiness
- Anxiety or panic attacks
- Irritability or rage
- Difficulty bonding with baby
- Intrusive thoughts
- Loss of interest in activities
- Sleep problems beyond baby's wake-ups

If either parent experiences these, seek professional help immediately. Postpartum mood disorders are medical conditions, not character failures.

Parenting As A Team

Successful co-parenting requires alignment on key issues:

Issue 1: Discipline Philosophy

Before children need discipline, discuss:
• What behaviours require discipline?
• What methods will you use (time-out, consequences, physical discipline)?
• How will you maintain consistency?
• What if you disagree in the moment?
• How will you present a united front?

On several occasions, I had disagreements with my ex-wife over child discipline. Early in the marriage, I would spank the children, but after some time, I decided it was the wrong approach but my wife disagreed and this continued leading to constant dispute between us.

Issue 2: Educational Choices

Decide together:
• Public, private, or home-school?
• What if we disagree?
• What values guide this decision?
• How much can we afford?
• What if the child has special needs?

These decisions often reveal values differences. One parent prioritizes academic excellence; the other prioritizes social development. Neither is wrong, but alignment is necessary.

Issue 3: Religious/Spiritual Upbringing

For religious couples:
• What faith will we teach?
• How involved will the children be in religious community?
• What if children reject our faith?
• How will we handle questions about other faiths?

For interfaith couples, this becomes even more complex. Revisit Chapter 10's discussion of raising children across faith traditions.

Issue 4: Screen Time and Technology

Modern parenting faces unique challenges:
• At what age should the child be given a phone?
• How much screen time?
• What content is acceptable?
• When does the child get a phone?
• Social media access and monitoring?
• Gaming rules?

Issue 5: Extended Family Involvement

How much will grandparents/relatives:
- Babysit or help with childcare?
- Influence parenting decisions?
- Have input on naming, education, and religion?
- Undermine your rules or spoil children?

Set boundaries early.

When Parenting Styles Clash

Even couples who discussed parenting theoretically face conflicts when dealing with actual children:

Clash 1: Permissive vs. Authoritarian

One parent is strict; the other is lenient.

The strict parent feels undermined and frustrated. The lenient parent thinks the strict one is too harsh. Children learn to play parents against each other.

Solution: Find a middle ground. Both extremes have problems. Aim for authoritative (firm but warm) parenting that both can implement.

Clash 2: Anxious vs. Relaxed

One parent worries constantly; the other is laid-back.

The anxious parent thinks the relaxed one is negligent. The relaxed parent thinks the anxious one is smothering.

Solution: Recognize that both perspectives are validity. Safety matters (anxious parent is right), but children need freedom to explore (relaxed parent is right). Divide domains—one handles medical/safety decisions, the other handles social/independence decisions.

Clash 3: Traditional Gender Roles vs. Equality

Oyèrónké Oyěwùmí cautions against interpreting African marriage systems solely through Western gender frameworks, noting that colonial lenses often distort indigenous understandings of power, responsibility, and relational roles (Oyěwùmí, 1997). One parent expects traditional division (mother nurtures, father provides); the other expects equality. This often reflects cultural upbringing and requires extensive negotiation.

Solution: Discuss what each wants and why. Find a compromise respecting both perspectives while meeting practical needs.

The Golden Rule of Parenting Conflicts:

Never disagree in front of children. Discuss privately, reach an agreement, present a united front. If you must disagree publicly, say,

"Mom/Dad and I will discuss this and let you know our decision." Children need parents who work together, not parents who undermine each other.

Childlessness: By Choice

Some couples might decide not to have children for the following reasons:
- Career and life goals incompatible with parenting
- Financial concerns
- Environmental/overpopulation concerns
- Don't feel parental desire
- Value freedom and flexibility
- Health concerns
- Bad experiences in their own childhood

Challenges Childfree Couples Face:

Challenge 1: Social Pressure

Particularly in traditional cultures, childless couples face:
- Constant questions: "When are you having children?"
- Assumptions that something is wrong
- Judgment and criticism
- Exclusion from family/community events
- Suspicion about motives

In some African cultures, family members attribute childlessness to the couple being caused cursed or to selfishness. They can't comprehend that they genuinely don't want children. They can't understand the distinction between bareness and deliberate decision not to have children.

Challenge 2: Pressure from Spouse's Family

Even if both spouses are aligned, family pressure:
- "Give us grandchildren."
- "You'll regret it later."
- "Who will care for you when you're old?"
- "Your marriage isn't complete without children."

Setting boundaries: "We appreciate your concern, but this decision is ours alone. We won't discuss it further."

Challenge 3: One Partner Changes Their Mind

Sometimes couples agree to be childfree, then one partner's feelings change: This situation has no easy answer. If one wants children and the other doesn't, someone will be deeply unhappy regardless of the choice.

For Couples Considering a Childfree Life:

Ask yourselves:

• Do we both genuinely not want children, or is one deferring to the other?

• Can we handle social pressure and judgment?

• What will give our lives meaning and purpose?

• What happens if one of us changes their mind?

• How will we handle regret if it arises?

If there's ambivalence, explore it thoroughly before deciding.

Childlessness: Not By Choice

This experience brings unique grief and challenge.

The Pain of Infertility:

Infertility creates stress through:

• Grief and loss

• Financial burden of treatments

• Physical pain and hormonal effects

• Sexual intimacy becoming clinical rather than intimate

• Disagreement about when to stop trying

• Blame (even unspoken)

• Seeing others easily achieve what you desperately want

• Isolation from friends with children

Navigating Infertility as a Couple:

Strategy 1: Grieve Together

Allow space for sadness, anger, disappointment. Don't minimize each other's pain or pressure each other to "stay positive."

Strategy 2: Make Decisions Together

Decide together:

• What treatments to pursue

• How much money to spend

• When to stop trying

• Whether to pursue adoption

• Whether to pursue surrogacy/donor options

• Whether to accept childlessness

No one should feel pressured into treatments they don't want or prevented from pursuing options they do want.

Strategy 3: Protect Your Sex Life

Don't let baby-making destroy intimacy. Have sex for connection and pleasure, not just for procreation. Take breaks from trying if needed to restore intimacy.

Strategy 4: Set Boundaries with Others

You don't owe anyone an explanations about your family planning. Practice saying:
- "We'd prefer not to discuss this."
- "This is a private matter."
- "We'll let you know if there's news to share."

Strategy 5: Seek Support

Find support through:
- Infertility counselling
- Support groups (online or in-person)
- Friends who've experienced it
- Therapists specializing in reproductive grief

Don't try to handle this alone.

Strategy 6: Consider All Options

Options beyond continued fertility treatments:
- Adoption (domestic or international)
- Foster care
- Surrogacy
- Donor eggs/sperm
- Accepting childlessness and building a meaningful life without children

None of these is the "right" answer. The right answer is what works for you as a couple.

When One Partner Wants to Keep Trying and the Other Doesn't:

This impasse is agonizing. One partner isn't ready to give up hope; the other is exhausted and ready to move on.

Consider:
- Setting a clear deadline or limit (financial, time-based, or number of attempts)
- Taking a break to reassess
- Each partner expressing what they need and why
- Counselling to process the different timelines

Finding Meaning After Infertility:

Whether you eventually have children through other means or remain childless, finding meaning matters:

The Impact On Marriage: Children Or No Children

Whether you have children or not, your marriage must remain the primary relationship:

For Parents:

Your children are temporary residents. Your spouse is (hopefully) permanent. Children will leave; your spouse should remain. Therefore:

- Don't sacrifice your marriage on the altar of perfect parenting
- Maintain date nights and couple time
- Support each other as partners, not just co-parents
- Remember you were a couple before you were parents

Many couples become so child-focused that they wake up at empty nest realizing they have nothing in common anymore. Prevent this by maintaining your marriage throughout parenting years.

For Childfree Couples:

Build a meaningful life that:

- Provides purpose beyond yourselves
- Creates community and connection
- Leaves a legacy (through work, mentorship, community service, creativity)
- Uses your freedom and resources intentionally

Reflection & Assessment

Personal Reflection

How has parenthood changed my priorities?

Have I unintentionally neglected my partner?

Partner Dialogue

How do we protect our relationship while raising children?

Where do we need better teamwork?

Reality Check (1–5)

Parenting alignment

Couple connection

Support balance

The Bottom Line

Whether you have children or not is a deeply personal choice with profound implications. What matters is:

- Both partners are aligned on the choice
- You're honest about your motivations and desires
- You prepare as much as possible for the realities
- You support each other through challenges
- You maintain your marriage as the primary relationship

Children can bring tremendous joy and meaning. They can also bring stress and challenge. The same marriage can thrive with or without children depending on how the couple navigates their choice. Choose intentionally. Prepare thoroughly. Support each other continuously.

CHAPTER 13: THE PLACE OF COMPROMISE

Silence is not peace — it is postponed conflict.

Finding Common Ground

Marriage is a continuous negotiation. Two complete individuals with different backgrounds, preferences, values, and visions must somehow create a shared life. This requires compromise—but not all compromise is created equal. Some compromises strengthen marriages; some slowly destroy them.

In many African communities, conflict was rarely treated as a private matter between two individuals alone. Elders, mediators, and witnesses were often involved—not to assign blame, but to restore harmony. The guiding question was not who was right, but how dignity, trust, and continuity could be preserved.

This chapter explores what healthy compromise looks like, what issues are non-negotiable, when to defer to your partner, and how to find middle ground without losing yourself.

Understanding Compromise

Let me start with what compromise is NOT:
• One partner always giving in
• Keeping score ("I compromised on this, so you owe me")
• Forcing someone to violate core values
• Pretending agreement when you fundamentally disagree
• Resentfully doing what your partner wants

Real compromise means:
• Both partners adjust from their ideal position
• Both partners feel the solution is fair enough to live with
• The relationship benefits even if neither gets exactly what they wanted
• No one feels coerced or defeated
• Future compromises don't reference past ones as debts

The Three Categories Of Issues

Not all issues are equal. Couples benefit from categorizing issues into three types:

Category 1: Preferences (Negotiable)

These are things you prefer but can live without:
- Restaurant choice
- Vacation destination
- Paint colour
- Social plans
- Minor household habits
- Entertainment choices

It should be easy to make compromises on preferences should be easy to compromise on. If you fight bitterly over every restaurant choice, the issue isn't the restaurant—it's power, control, or unresolved resentment.

You can take turns choosing. One week, she picks the restaurant. Next week, you pick. Occasionally choose something the other wouldn't select, but agree to try each other's choices with a good attitude. It works because neither of you always have their way.

Category 2: Values (Somewhat Negotiable)

These matter more than preferences but aren't absolute:
- How clean should the house be?
- How much time to spend with extended family?
- How to spend leisure time?
- Career ambitions
- Social life intensity
- Pet preferences

Values require genuine compromises—both partners adjusting to find a workable middle ground. Example: One partner values a spotless home; the other is comfortable with a "lived-in" mess. Compromise might be: shared spaces stay clean, personal spaces are each person's responsibility, and a weekly cleaning day ensures baseline cleanliness.

Category 3: Core Values/Non-Negotiables (Not Negotiable)

These are fundamental to your identity and wellbeing:
- Whether to have children
- Religious practice and beliefs
- Fidelity and faithfulness
- Honesty and trust
- Treatment of family
- Life purpose and calling

• Major life decisions (where to live, career changes)

Core values shouldn't be compromised away. If your core values are incompatible, you may be fundamentally unsuited as partners. The key is correctly identifying which category an issue falls into. Many conflicts arise because partners miscategorise—treating preferences as core values, or dismissing actual values as mere preferences.

When To Compromise

Compromise makes sense when:

Situation 1: Both Positions Have Merit

You want to live in the city for career opportunities and culture. Your spouse wants suburbs for space and good schools. Both are valid. Compromise might be: suburbs with easy city access, or city for now with plan to move when children arrive.

Situation 2: The Issue Matters More to One Partner

It's somewhat important to you but critical to your spouse. Defer to them. A spouse desperately wanted a dog and the other was ambivalent who didn't dislike dogs but didn't want the responsibility, but compromised because it mattered so much to the partner. Fifteen years later, she loved that dog. Sometimes the right compromise leads you somewhere you didn't know you'd want to go.

Situation 3: You Can Find Creative Solutions

Instead of A or B, you discover option C that incorporates elements of both. One couple wanted different vacation styles—he wanted adventure, she wanted relaxation. Compromise: trips that include both (hiking mornings, beach afternoons, or alternating active and relaxing days).

Situation 4: Relationship Health Matters More Than Being Right

Sometimes you compromise not because your partner is right but because being together in harmony matters more than winning this particular point. A spouse wanted to spend Christmas with her family and the other wanted to start his own traditions. He compromised and went to her family. Was he right that they should establish their own traditions? Yes. But his relationship with his parents mattered, and being together peacefully mattered more than being right.

When Not To Compromise

Some situations don't call for compromise:

Situation 1: It Violates Your Core Values

If compromising requires you to betray fundamental values, don't do it. One Christian woman refused to compromise on attending church despite her non-religious husband's preference that she stop. Her faith was core to her identity. She found middle ground (not pressuring him to attend, not making their social life entirely church-based) but didn't compromise on her own practice.

Situation 2: It Harms Your Physical or Mental Health

If what your partner wants damages your wellbeing, that's not compromise territory. One man's wife wanted him to work 80-hour weeks to maximize income. This was destroying his health and mental state. He refused to compromise on working himself to death, even though it meant a lower household income.

Situation 3: It Involves Abuse or Mistreatment

Never compromise on being treated with respect, dignity, and kindness. If your partner demands that you accept abusive behaviour, the answer is no, this is not up for negotiation.

Situation 4: It Requires Losing Your Identity

Some partners want you to fundamentally change who you are. This isn't a compromise; it's erasure. A husband wanted a spouse to stop seeing her friends, quit her job, dress differently, and change her personality. He said marriage requires compromise. But what he wanted wasn't compromise—it was her becoming someone else entirely.

Situation 5: It's Always One-Sided

If you're always the one compromising and your partner never bends, the relationship is unbalanced. True compromise requires both partners to adjust sometimes. If only one person compromises, that's not compromise—that's one person controlling and the other person surrendering.

How To Compromise Effectively

Step 1: Clarify What You Actually Want and Why

Before negotiating, understand your own position:
- What specifically do I want?
- Why does this matter to me?
- What core need or value does this serve?
- How important is this (1-10 scale)?
- What would I need to feel okay about a compromise?

Step 2: Understand Your Partner's Position

Ask and truly listen:
- What do you want?
- Why does this matter to you?
- What core need or value does this serve?
- How important is this to you (1-10 scale)?
- What would you need to feel okay about a compromise?

Often, understanding the "why" makes compromise easier. You might think you're fighting about where to spend Thanksgiving, but really you're negotiating feelings of family loyalty, traditions, and belonging.

Step 3: Look for Underlying Needs

Often the stated position isn't the real need.

Example: Wife wants to spend a specific amount on redecorating. Husband resists. They're not really fighting about money—she wants to feel at home in their space (need: comfort and self-expression), and he wants financial security (need: safety and control).

Solution addressing both needs: A modest redecorating budget that improves her comfort without threatening his security.

Step 4: Generate Multiple Options

Don't get stuck on A vs. B. Brainstorm:
- Can we do both?
- Can we do neither and find option C?
- Can we do yours now and mine later?
- Can we each get part of what we want?
- What creative solution serves both our needs?

Step 5: Test the Compromise

Before committing permanently:
- Try it for a defined period
- Agree to revisit and adjust if needed
- Check in about how it's working
- Be willing to renegotiate

For example: Agree to a three-month trial. Try the compromise for three months, then evaluate. If it's not working, renegotiate. This makes compromise less scary because you know you can adjust.

Step 6: Let Go of Resentment

Once you agree to a compromise, commit to it fully. Don't bring it up in future fights or hold it over your partner's head. If you find yourself unable to let go of resentment, the compromise may not have been fair. Renegotiate before resentment poisons your relationship.

Compromise In Action: Real Examples

Let me share how real couples navigated specific compromise situations:

Example 1: Career Relocation

Situation: He received a job offer requiring a move across country. She had career and community ties where they lived.

Bad compromise: He takes the job; she resentfully follows, sacrificing her career.

Good compromise: They negotiated: He takes the job with the agreement that next career decision prioritizes her, they visit her family/friends quarterly at company expense, and they'll move back to her preferred location within five years. Both sacrificed something; both gained something.

Example 2: Extended Family Involvement

Situation: His mother wanted to drop by unannounced constantly. She wanted privacy and boundaries.

Bad compromise: She accepts an intrusive mother-in-law and grows increasingly resentful.

Good compromise: They established that Mother-in-law visits weekly but calls first, has her own key for emergencies only, and they have one family dinner monthly. She gets regular access; wife gets privacy.

Example 3: Social Life Differences

Situation: He's extremely introverted and wants quiet weekends. She's extroverted and wants an active social life.

Bad compromise: He forces himself to socialize constantly and becomes depleted, or she never sees friends and feels isolated.

Good compromise: She goes out with friends some evenings/weekends while he has solo time. They have one scheduled social event together monthly. One night each week is dedicated to couple time. Both get their needs met without either being miserable.

Example 4: Housework Division

Situation: Both work full-time, but she does 80% of the housework. He's comfortable with a messier home; she needs cleanliness.

Bad compromise: She continues doing everything while he does nothing.

Good compromise: They created an explicit division: He handles certain tasks (dishes, trash, laundry), she handles others (cooking, bathroom cleaning). Areas he manages can be messier; areas she manages stay clean. Baseline cleanliness is maintained through weekly cleaning session together.

Example 5: Different Parenting Styles

Situation: She's anxious about child safety; he's more relaxed.

Bad compromise: She micromanages every decision and he feels side-lined, or he ignores her concerns and she feels unheard.

Good compromise: They divided domains—she makes decisions about medical care, nutrition, car seats, safety equipment (her anxiety serves the child well here). He makes decisions about age-appropriate independence, social activities, and risk-taking play (his relaxed approach serves the child well here). Both trust the other's domain.

The Power Of Deferring

Sometimes the best "compromise" is one partner deferring to the other because:

- It matters more to them
- They have more expertise
- It's their domain
- You genuinely don't care

One couple's wisdom: "We each have domains where we defer to the other. She handles anything related to our children's education because she cares more and knows more. I handle anything related to home maintenance and technology. For most issues in our respective domains, the other partner defers. This prevents constant negotiation over everything."

Healthy deferring requires:

- The one who defers does so genuinely, not resentfully
- The one making decisions doesn't abuse the power
- Domains are roughly equal in importance and effort
- Both partners can request renegotiation if needed

When Compromise Fails

Always remember Respect in The Three Pillars in conflict resolution (See Chapter 1). Sometimes you genuinely cannot find an acceptable compromise:

Option 1: Table It

"We're stuck on this. Let's take a break and revisit in a week with a fresh perspective." Time often brings clarity or creative solutions.

Option 2: Seek External Input

Get perspective from:
• Trusted friends or family
• Counsellor or therapist
• Religious leader
• Financial advisor (for money issues)
• Parenting expert (for child-related issues)
Outside perspective often reveals solutions you couldn't see.

Option 3: Trial and Error

"Let's try your way for three months, then my way for three months, and see what works better." Empirical testing often resolves theoretical disagreements.

Option 4: Accept That This Is a Difference

Some differences just are. You have different politics, different decorating tastes, and different friend groups. Acknowledge and accept rather than endlessly trying to change each other. He supports one party; she supports another. They have voted against each other for decades. They have accepted this difference. They don't discuss politics because they will never agree. Their marriage is more important than political alignment.

Option 5: Recognize Incompatibility

You may discover you're fundamentally incompatible on something critical. If you cannot compromise and cannot live with the difference, you may need to end the relationship. Although this is heart-breaking, it is but sometimes necessary. Better to acknowledge incompatibility than spend decades in miserable compromise.

Cultural Differences In Compromise

Different approaches to compromise:
Many African cultures emphasize:
• Deference to age, authority, and tradition
• Collective decision-making involving extended family
• Men having final say in certain domains
• Women having authority in household management
• Less emphasis on individual fulfilment in marriage
Western culture emphasizes:
• Equal partnership and negotiation
• Individual fulfilment as marriage goal
• Less deference to tradition or authority
• More resistance to gender-based role divisions
• Privacy in marital decision-making

Neither approach is inherently superior, but cross-cultural couples must navigate these different frameworks explicitly. One partner was raised that husbands lead. The other was raised that couples are equal partners. Create your own model—one provides vision and leadership in some areas, the other provides it in others, and negotiate major decisions together as equals. It's not traditional African or traditional Western; it's yours.

Reflection & Assessment

Personal Reflection
> Where have I over-compromised?
> Where have I been unwilling to bend?

Partner Dialogue
> What feels fair in our relationship?
> Where does compromise feel one-sided?

Reality Check
> ☐ Compromise is mutual
> ☐ Compromise is unequal

The Bottom Line On Compromise

Healthy compromise:
- Involves both partners adjusting
- Serves the relationship, not just one person
- Respects core values while negotiating preferences
- Creates solutions both can live with
- Doesn't build resentment
- Is revisited and renegotiated as needed

Unhealthy compromise:
- Is always one-sided
- Requires violating values
- Builds resentment
- Feels coerced
- Creates winners and losers
- Never changes despite problems

Marriage is a continuous dance of give-and-take. Learn to compromise well, know when to defer, understand your non-negotiables, and remember that being together in harmony often matters more than having your way.

In the next chapter, we'll explore one of the most controversial topics: different family structures, specifically comparing polygamy and monogamy based on personal experience.

CHAPTER 14: POLYGAMY VS. MONOGAMY

*Polygamy, like monogamy, succeeds or fails not by structure
alone, but by the maturity of those within it.*

Personal Journey, Cultural Context, and Honest Reflection

This is perhaps the most personal chapter in this book. I grew up in a polygamous household in Nigeria, experiencing first-hand a family structure most Western readers find incomprehensible or morally wrong. I now live in a monogamous marriage. This unique perspective allows me to discuss both systems honestly, acknowledging the strengths and weaknesses of each without dismissing either entirely.

Polygamy remains prevalent in parts of Africa due to a combination of historical, economic, cultural, and religious influences. Traditionally, many African societies viewed marriage not merely as a union between two individuals but as a strategic alliance between families and clans. In some regions, religious traditions—particularly within certain interpretations of Islam and customary law—have further legitimised the practice. However, contemporary African societies are increasingly diverse in their views. Urbanisation, education, women's economic participation, and evolving legal frameworks have significantly reduced the prevalence of polygamous unions in many countries.

My father had his own reasons for marrying more than one wife. He was the only surviving child of his parents and felt alone and lonely. According to him, his children served as his brothers and sisters, whom he didn't have and didn't want his children to experience the loneliness he experienced.

Let me be clear from the start: I am not advocating for polygamy or monogamy. I chose monogamy for my own life, and I believe it's the better system for me in my contexts. But I also can't pretend polygamy is purely oppressive or dysfunctional, because I witnessed both dysfunction and genuine love in my father's household. This chapter will be uncomfortable for some readers. That's okay. Sometimes the truth is uncomfortable.

My Polygamous Childhood

My father had four wives. My mother was the third wife and he married her as a widow. He married the last two women including my mother as widows. It was common in my culture, for the deceased male relatives to marry their brother's wives to ensure the welfare of the widow and the deceased children. I am the only child my parents had together, though I had several half-siblings on both sides. We all lived in the same compound with each wife having her own dwelling within it. This was not unusual in my community. Polygamy was legal, culturally accepted, and in some ways expected for men who could afford to support multiple wives and many children.

What I Observed:

The Complexity:

Life in a polygamous household defies simple characterization. Some of what I witnessed:

My father genuinely cared for all his wives, though I believe he loved the most senior wife (she was his first love). He provided financially for all households, settled disputes, and spent time with each family unit.

The wives had complex relationships. Sometimes they cooperated and supported each other, particularly in child-rearing and household management. At other times, they competed for my father's attention, resources, and favour.

The children navigated complicated sibling relationships. Some siblings from different mothers were close. Others were rivals. Birth order mattered, but which mother you came from mattered more.

Resources were never quite equal. My father tried to be fair, but his attention, his money, and his favour were finite. There was always underlying competition.

The Challenges I Witnessed:

Growing up in a polygamous family. I witnessed jealousy (See Introduction). Even when wives genuinely tried to rise above it, the structure itself generated jealousy. When my father spent the night in one wife's dwelling, the others felt excluded. When he distributed foodstuffs, they were scrutinized for fairness.

Children suffered from the competition. We learned to advocate for our own mothers and their interests. We picked up on adult tensions and took sides. The family functioned more like competing units than one unified whole.

The junior wives (second, third, and fourth) occupied a lower social status. Despite my father's efforts at equality, there was a hierarchy. The first wife had more influence and respect.

Financial strain was real. Supporting four households meant resources were stretched. All wives and children had enough, but none had plenty. A family of similar size in monogamous structure might have been more financially comfortable.

Emotional strain on my father was visible. He worked constantly to keep peace, show fairness, and meet everyone's needs. The burden of maintaining four marriages was heavy.

The Advantages I Witnessed:

Built-in support system among wives. When one was sick, others helped with her children. When one had a conflict with my father, others sometimes mediated.

More hands for childcare and household management. Several adults watched over the children. Work was distributed among the wives.

Less pressure on any one wife to meet all of my father's needs. If one wife was unwell, tired, or unavailable, others stepped in.

A large family meant never being alone. We had many siblings to play with, learn from, and support us. The compound was always alive with activity.

My father had multiple and varied companionships. (I include this not to endorse it but to acknowledge that from his perspective, this was an advantage.)

My Honest Assessment:

Polygamy can work when:
• There are abundant resources to support all wives and children adequately
• Cultural norms and legal requirements support the practice (it's not seen as deviant or wrong)
• All parties entered willingly and with full understanding
• The husband is exceptionally fair, wise, and attentive
• Wives have genuine autonomy and support
• Children are not pitted against each other

But even in best-case scenarios, polygamy has inherent problems:
• Human nature struggles with sharing an intimate partnership
• Resources and attention are divided
• Competition is built into the structure
• The well-being of the children is complicated by divided loyalties
• Wives' status is inherently unequal

Why I Chose Monogamy

Given my upbringing, people sometimes ask why I chose monogamous marriage. Several reasons:

Reason 1: What I Witnessed

Despite some positives, I saw the pain polygamy caused my mother. I watched my mother suffer isolation, loneliness and conflicts with other wives which eventually led to divorce. I saw jealousy corrode relationships. Competition for my father's attention and resources amongst the wives was fierce. I experienced sibling rivalry intensified by having different mothers. I witnessed the financial and emotional strain on my father. I decided I didn't want to create that complexity in my own life.

Reason 2: Religious Conviction

My religious faith taught me that marriage is better between one man and one woman, lifetime commitment except under strict conditions which are almost impossible to fulfil is polygamy allowed. This shaped my values.

Reason 3: What I Want in Marriage

I wanted a partnership—one woman to build a life with, to share everything with, to grow old with. I wanted depth and exclusivity in my marriage. Polygamy, by its nature, divides attention and intimacy.

Reason 4: Respect For My Wife

The woman I married would not have thrived under polygamy and did not want one. Although we did not discuss this before getting married and she could not have stopped me from marrying more than one wife. She wanted exclusive commitment, and I wanted her more than I wanted the option of additional wives.

Reason 5: Attention And Care For My Children

I wanted to give all my attention and love to my children. Doing so meant fewer children. Growing up, I craved for the love and attention of my father The love he had for me was never in doubt, but I did not get as much attention as I would have liked due to his divided attention and the competition for his love and attention by many other children.

The Case For Monogamy

Based on my experience:

Benefit 1: Focused Intimacy

All your intimate energy—emotional, physical, spiritual—goes to one person. This allows deep knowledge, profound connection, and growth together that's difficult with divided attention, although this is not guaranteed. The fact is that I could barely manage one relationship well which would make it difficult to navigate multiple.

Benefit 2: Simpler Family Dynamics

One household, two parents, shared children. No competing interests among wives or divided loyalties among children. Resources go to one family unit.

Benefit 3: Equality in Partnership

While monogamy doesn't guarantee equality, the structure allows for true partnership between equals. Polygamy inherently creates hierarchy.

Benefit 4: Less Jealousy

Jealousy still exists in monogamy (over time, attention, external attractions), but the structure doesn't require you to share your spouse's intimate partnership with others.

Benefit 5: Clear Commitment

The exclusivity of monogamy means clear, total commitment. You've chosen each other, forsaking all others. This clarity has psychological and emotional benefits.

Benefit 6: Practical and Legal Simplicity

In most modern contexts, monogamy is legally recognized, socially accepted, and practically simpler. Inheritance, insurance, medical decisions, and custody—all are straightforward in a monogamous marriage.

The Case For Polygamy

As understood in its cultural context, I want to be fair to the system I was raised in, even though I didn't choose it:

Argument 1: Cultural And Legal Appropriateness

In contexts where polygamy is normative, it functions within that cultural and legal framework. Women enter polygamous marriages understanding the structure. Men take on the responsibilities of multiple households. The community and government support and regulate the practice. Imposing Western monogamous standards on every culture is itself a kind of cultural imperialism and problematic.

Argument 2: Practical Benefits in Certain Contexts

In societies without strong social safety nets, polygamy can provide:

* Security for widows (marrying the deceased brother's widow)
* Protection for unmarried women in male-dominated societies
* Support for women in cultures where unmarried women are vulnerable
* Shared childcare and household labour
* Large family networks providing mutual support

Argument 3: Gender Ratio Realities

In some contexts (post-war societies, areas with high male mortality), women significantly outnumber men. Polygamy ensures more women have access to marriage and its benefits (in societies where women depend on marriage for survival and social status).

Argument 4: Honest About Male Nature

Some argue polygamy is being honest about male sexual/romantic nature—many men are attracted to multiple women. Polygamy formalizes this with responsibility and commitment rather than hiding it in secret affairs and abandoned mistresses.

Argument 5: Financial Security for Women

In some contexts, women choose polygamy. They prefer being a co-wife in a stable, well-resourced household over being a solo wife in poverty or being unmarried.

Problems With Both Systems

Let me be honest: Both systems have problems.

Monogamy's Problems:

Monogamy creates:

* Intense pressure on one person to meet all needs
* Boredom and stagnation if couples don't actively nurture the relationship
* Vulnerability to affairs when needs aren't met
* Potential for domestic violence and abuse behind closed doors
* Isolation if extended family, community and government support is lacking
* High divorce rates in modern societies where monogamy is practiced

Monogamy isn't automatically healthier or better—it must be worked at intentionally.

Polygamy's Problems:

Polygamy creates:

* Inevitable unhealthy comparison and competition among wives
* Diluted attention and resources

- Complicated children's relationships
- Systematic inequality (even a benevolent hierarchy is still a hierarchy)
- Jealousy is built into the structure
- Potential for favouritism and abuse

Even well-managed polygamy has inherent structural problems.

The Uncomfortable Truth

Here's what makes people uncomfortable: Some polygamous marriages are happy and functional. Some monogamous marriages are miserable and dysfunctional. The structure of marriage matters, but it's not everything. What matters more:

- Commitment and faithfulness within whatever structure you've chosen
- Respect and kindness toward partners
- Fair distribution of resources and responsibilities
- Healthy conflict resolution
- Supporting children's wellbeing
- Personal integrity and character

I've known people in polygamous marriages who were content and people in monogamous marriages who were miserable. I've also seen the reverse. Structure matters. Character matters more. A woman I spoke to who is currently in a polygamous relationship said to me:

But I love the setup because I love having the idea of a best friend who is a co-wife….. I really want that. Just a big happy family. I want."

On the downside, she said: *I want that but it's very had to have that when you have a weak husband and no money.* She said further *On my side, I decided that I don't want a relationship with my co-wife because I felt that she is a bully.*

My Final Take:

Despite my nuanced perspective, let me be clear: For most people in most modern contexts, they choose monogamy because:
- It allows focused intimacy and deep partnership
- It's simpler practically and legally
- It better supports equality between partners
- It doesn't require navigating structural jealousy
- It's better for children's emotional development
- It's more sustainable in modern economic contexts

If you're from a polygamous cultural background and considering your options, I encourage you to carefully examine whether polygamy serves your values and goals or whether you're simply following tradition.

If you're in a polygamous marriage:
- Take seriously the responsibility to be scrupulously fair
- Provide adequately for all wives and children
- Don't pit wives or children against each other
- Acknowledge the pain it create, even with good intentions
- Ensure all wives have autonomy and rights
- Support children's relationships across maternal lines
- Accept that this structure has inherent challenges

And think of the following before making a final decision in whichever one you choose:
- Are you equipped emotionally, financially, and practically for this?
- Have you thoroughly examined your motivations?
- Are all parties entering with full understanding and consent?
- Can you provide adequately for multiple households?
- Are you prepared for the inevitable complications?
- Is this the life you genuinely want, or are you following cultural or societal expectations?
- Have you considered monogamy seriously as an alternative?

Reflection & Assessment

Personal Reflection

How have culture and upbringing shaped my views here?
What structure genuinely aligns with my values?

Partner Dialogue

Are we aligned on the relationship structure?

Have assumptions replaced honest conversation?
Reality Check

☐ Values aligned

☐ Values conflicted

The Bottom Line

A friend of mine, with whom I discussed this topic, summed it up very succinctly when he said:

I must quickly point out that neither of the two types is outrightly good or bad. It all depends on individual preferences and the prevailing laws in the country of residence. For me, I have seen the best and worst of both marriages — either early in their marital stages or later at very old ages.

I grew up in polygamy. I chose monogamy. This isn't a condemnation of my father or my family—it's an acknowledgment that different structures suit different contexts. But in modern contexts with emphasis on individual rights, gender equality, and partnership marriage, monogamy seems to be a better fit. Whatever structure you choose, commit to it fully. Honour your commitments. Treat your partner(s) with respect. Support your children.

Build something meaningful.

Structure matters. But love, respect, commitment, and character matter more.

CHAPTER 15: SINGLE PARENTHOOD

Raising a child alone demands twice the strength and twice the grace.

Challenges, Strengths, and Survival

According to **Statistics South Africa's General Household Survey (2023),** approximately **42% of children in South Africa live with only one parent**, and the overwhelming majority of these households are headed by women. The pattern is not unique to South Africa. According to the **U.S. Census Bureau (2023),** approximately **23% of children under the age of 18 live with one parent and no other adult present,** one of the highest rates of single-parent households among developed nations. The majority of these households are headed by mothers.

Behind every percentage point is a parent navigating the emotional weight of responsibility alone: managing finances, discipline, schooling, and personal healing while attempting to maintain stability for children. Understanding the scale of single-parent households helps shift the conversation from stigma to structure. It reminds us that healing after divorce is not only about personal recovery—it is about rebuilding a family system under new conditions. And where there are children, the work of emotional health becomes even more urgent.

Single parenthood wasn't part of the original plan for most people. Whether through divorce, death, or unplanned circumstances, single parents face unique challenges while raising children alone. This chapter acknowledges the difficulties while celebrating the resilience and strength single parents demonstrate daily. Single parents face an immeasurable trust deficit in new relationships. Our data shows single parents trust their partners at rates 10-12 percentage points lower than non-single parents—a pattern consistent across both continents.

This trust gap—remarkably consistent whether in Lagos or Los Angeles—likely reflects protective instincts developed through past relationship failures. Understanding this dynamic helps both single parents and their partners navigate trust-building with appropriate patience.

Challenges of single parenthood:
- Financial strain
- Time management and exhaustion
- Lack of parenting backup
- Guilt and self-doubt
- Difficulty dating or finding new a relationship
- Feeling judged by others
- Balancing work and parenting
- Children's emotional/behavioural issues

Reported Strengths:
- Closer relationship with children
- Personal growth and resilience
- Freedom to make decisions without conflict
- Pride in managing alone
- Children learning independence earlier

How People Become Single Parents

Path 1: Divorce

Most single parents reach this status through divorce. They entered marriage expecting partnership, and it ended. The transition to single parenthood after divorce is complicated by:
- Processing grief and anger about marriage failure
- Coordinating custody and co-parenting with someone you may not trust or respect
- In some instances, financial burden borne by one person instead of two and maintaining two households
- Children's emotional adjustment to divorce
- Dating and new relationships while parenting

Path 2: Never Married

Some single parents never married the other parent:
- Unplanned pregnancy outside of committed relationship
- Relationship ended during pregnancy or shortly after birth
- One partner unwilling to commit to marriage
- Cultural or religious reasons preventing marriage

These single parents face unique challenges:
- Establishing paternity and custody legally
- No prior partnership to reference
- Often younger and less financially established

- Family and community judgment
- Uncertainty about the other parent's involvement

Path 3: Widowhood

Losing a spouse to death creates a different single-parent experience:

- Grieving while parenting
- Children grieving the lost parent
- Financial impact (though sometimes insurance helps)
- Permanent finality (unlike divorce, there's no co-parenting)
- Community sympathy rather than judgment
- Preserving deceased parent's memory for children

Path 4: Abandonment or Incarceration

Some single parents functionally parent alone because the other parent is:

- Incarcerated long-term
- Addicted and non-functional
- Mentally ill and unable to parent
- Simply absent with no contact

These situations create ambiguity:

- Technically not a single parent but practically functioning as one
- Explaining parent's absence to children
- Holding space for possible return or having to accept permanence
- Financial and emotional impact of partner's issues

The Challenges Of Single Parenthood

Challenge 1: Financial Strain

Single-income households supporting children face enormous financial pressure:

- Housing costs designed for two incomes
- Childcare costs (single parents can't tag-team)
- Health insurance and medical costs
- Reduced earning potential (can't work unlimited hours due to parenting)
- No financial backup for emergencies

Challenge 2: Time Poverty

Single parents have no backup. Every childcare need, every appointment, every school event, every illness—all falls on one person.

Challenge 3: Lack of Adult Support and Companionship

Parenting is isolating even with a partner. Single parenting can be profoundly lonely:
- No adult to debrief with about the day
- No one to validate your parenting decisions
- No one to celebrate small victories
- No physical affection or intimacy
- Limited social life due to parenting responsibilities

Challenge 4: Decision-Making Burden

Every parenting decision is yours alone:
- Medical decisions
- Educational choices
- Discipline approaches
- Screen time rules
- Friend and activity approvals
- Big life changes

Challenge 5: Guilt

Single parents carry enormous guilt:
- Guilt that children don't have two-parent household
- Guilt about not being enough
- Guilt about working and missing time with children
- Guilt about being tired and impatient
- Guilt about financial limitations
- Guilt about dating (time away from children, introducing new relationships)

Challenge 6: Exhaustion

Physical, mental, and emotional exhaustion is the single-parent baseline:
- All household labour falls on one person
- All parenting falls on one person
- All income-earning falls on one person
- All emotional labour falls to one person
- No breaks, no time off

Challenge 7: Social Isolation and Judgment

Single parents often face:
- Social exclusion from couple-dominated communities
- Judgment from married parents
- Assumptions about their character or choices
- Limited time for friendships and social connections
- Feeling like they don't fit anywhere

The Strengths of Single Parenthood

Despite the challenges, single parents reported unexpected benefits:

Benefit 1: Independence and Autonomy

No arguing about parenting decisions. No compromising with someone whose values differ. Your rules, your way.

Benefit 2: Closer Parent-Child Relationships
- Children see parent working hard for family
- More communication and honesty
- Children and parent are a team
- Shared experiences and adversity strengthen bonds

Benefit 3: Personal Growth

Single parents develop:
- Resilience
- Problem-solving skills
- Time management abilities
- Financial savvy
- Emotional strength
- Independence

Benefit 4: Modelling Resilience for Children

Children of single parents see:
- Hard work and perseverance
- Overcoming adversity
- Balancing multiple responsibilities
- Independence and self-sufficiency

Benefit 5: Freedom from Toxic Relationship

For single parents who left harmful relationships:
- Safety and peace
- No more walking on eggshells
- No more conflict and tension in the home
- Healthier environment for children
- Opportunity to heal and rebuild

Practical Strategies For Single Parents

Strategy 1: Build Your Village

You can't do this alone. Create support systems:
- Family who can help with childcare, meals, and emergencies
- Friends who understand and support
- Other single parents to relate to and help each other

- Community resources (religious, community centre, programs)
- Professional help when needed (therapist, financial advisor)

Strategy 2: Establish Routines and Systems

Structure prevents chaos:
- Consistent schedules for meals, homework, bedtime
- Meal planning and prep
- Cleaning systems
- Homework stations
- Organized spaces

Strategy 3: Lower Standards Where You Can

Perfect is not possible. Let go of:
- Spotless house (aim for clean enough)
- Elaborate meals (focus on nutritious ones)
- Perfect attendance at every child activity (prioritize what matters most)
- Looking put-together constantly (comfortable is fine)
- Pinterest-level parenting (functional is good enough)

Strategy 4: Take Care of Yourself

Self-care isn't selfish—it's survival:
- Sleep when you can
- Eat properly
- Exercise (even briefly)
- Take breaks when possible
- Maintain friendships
- Do something you enjoy occasionally

Strategy 5: Communicate Honestly with Children

The Three Pillars are also important in communicating with children (See Chapter 1) and:
- Acknowledge the situation
- Answer questions honestly
- Don't burden them with adult problems
- Don't badmouth the other parent
- Reassure them they're loved and safe
- Let them express emotions

Strategy 6: Seek Help When Needed

Don't suffer in silence:
- Financial assistance programs if needed
- Counselling for you and/or children
- Parenting classes or support groups
- Legal help for custody/support issues
- Medical care for physical/mental health

Strategy 7: Celebrate Small Victories
Acknowledge what you're accomplishing:
• Kids fed and safe? Victory.
• Made it through the day? Victory.
• Kid's homework done? Victory.
• Everyone has clean underwear? Victory.
Single parenting is hard. Celebrate what you're achieving.

Navigating Co-Parenting

For single parents who share custody:
Keys to Functional Co-Parenting:
• Put children's needs above your feelings about ex-partner
• Communicate about children's needs, not relationship failures
• Be consistent with rules and schedules across households
• Don't badmouth the other parent to the children
• Don't use children as messengers or spies
• Attend important events together when possible
• Support children's relationship with the other parent
When Co-Parenting is Impossible:
Sometimes the other parent is:
• Absent or completely uninvolved
• Unsafe (abusive, addicted, dangerous)
• Undermining (actively working against you)
In these cases:
• Document everything legally
• Establish clear custody and boundaries
• Protect your children
• Get legal help if needed
• Focus on what you can control
• Let go of trying to make co-parenting work with an unwilling/unable partner
Dating As A Single Parent
Many single parents want romantic relationships but face unique challenges:
Challenges:
• Limited time and energy for dating
• Children's needs come first
• Complicated to introduce children to new partners
• Potential partners may not want involvement with someone with children

- Guilt about time away from children
- Vetting potential partners carefully for children's safety

Guidelines:
- Take your time before introducing partners to children
- Be clear about being a parent from the start
- Date only people who respect your parenting responsibilities
- Listen to children's concerns about your dating
- Don't sacrifice parenting for relationships
- Remember you deserve companionship and love

Reflection & Assessment

Personal Reflection

How has single parenthood reshaped my identity?

Where do I need more support?

Reality Check (1–5)

Emotional support

Practical support

Self-care

The Bottom Line On Single Parenthood

Single parenting is not ideal. It's not what most people choose. It's hard—financially, emotionally, practically. But single parents are not failures. They are not broken. They are people navigating difficult circumstances while raising the next generation. They deserve respect, support, and recognition. If you're a single parent:
- You're doing better than you think
- Your children will remember your love and effort
- It gets easier (eventually)
- You're stronger than you know
- You're not alone

If you're partnered:
- Support the single parents in your life
- Don't judge
- Offer practical help
- Recognize their strength
- Appreciate your partnership

Single parenthood is one of the hardest jobs anyone can have. Those doing it deserve our admiration, not our judgment.

Scan this code for a short reflection related to Part IV.

PART V - CHALLENGES AND SOLUTIONS

External influences significantly impact relationship health. Family pressure, societal expectations, and religious communities all play roles, though their relative importance differs by culture. African respondents more consistently acknowledge external influences: 52% rate family background as important in partner selection versus 31% of Americans. Similarly, societal expectations ("Society") appear more frequently as a factor keeping unhappy African couples together.

Communication challenges emerge indirectly in the data. When respondents describe what they dislike about partners, American responses reveal communication themes: "Never there," "Double standards," "We don't always share the same values," and "Not enough attentiveness." African responses, while coded differently, suggest similar underlying dynamics through categories like "Other" that may encompass communication issues.

The data suggests a counselling opportunity: approximately 15-16% of respondents report unhappiness, while 20-24% would leave if given the option. The 5-8 percentage point gap represents couples who are unhappy but not actively planning exits—precisely the population most likely to benefit from professional intervention before minor issues become major crises.

Pause for Reflection

This part of *The Second Bridge* is designed to be read as a whole. Before moving to the next section, you are invited to pause and reflect on the ideas explored across all the chapters in this part.

A short reflection questionnaire is available to help you assess insights, patterns, and areas for growth.

Please complete the questionnaire only after reading all chapters in this part. (Scan the code at the end of this section to access the reflection.)

CHAPTER 16: RELATIONSHIP INFLUENCERS — EXTERNAL FORCES

*If you do not guard your marriage, the world will shape it
for you.*

Every relationship is shaped not only by the people in it, but also by the world around them. External forces—family, friends, work, culture, and technology—quietly influence behaviour, expectations, and emotional reactions. Understanding these forces allows couples to respond intentionally rather than react unconsciously.

Family and Friends

Family and friends often hold a powerful influence on relationships, especially in cultures where extended families are deeply involved in daily life. Their support can strengthen a relationship, but their involvement can also lead to tension if boundaries are unclear.

Family influence becomes problematic when couples depend too heavily on external approval or when relatives become involved in private · disagreements. Many marital conflicts intensify because partners discuss sensitive issues with those who may take sides or offer biased counsel.

Healthy couples recognise when family input is helpful and when it becomes intrusive. This requires the maturity to honour family while protecting the primary relationship. Family influence becomes harmful when:

• Private issues are shared widely and repeatedly
• Relatives attempt to shape decisions meant for the couple
• One partner seeks validation outside rather than inside the relationship
• Family loyalty conflicts with marital unity

Social Media and Technology

Technology has rapidly become one of the most influential external forces in modern relationships. While it offers connection and convenience, it also creates distraction, comparison, and emotional distance.

Excessive screen time reduces meaningful conversation. Online interactions can become emotional substitutes. Social media exposes couples to unrealistic portrayals of relationships, often creating dissatisfaction with reality.

Technology influences relationships through:
- Continuous distraction during daily interactions
- Online friendships that blur emotional boundaries
- Over-sharing personal issues publicly
- Heightened comparison with other couples
- Reduced time for genuine connection

Couples who thrive are those who consciously manage their digital environment. They remain transparent, protect private matters, and ensure technology does not replace presence.

Work and Career Pressures

Work can enrich a relationship by providing financial stability and personal growth. Yet the same work can drain a relationship when ambition, stress, or long hours overshadow emotional connection.

Many partners unintentionally give the best of themselves to their career which leaves them almost always too exhausted to properly connect with their partners. Over time, this creates emotional distance.

,Career pressure shows up through:
- Irregular schedules and limited shared time
- Work-related stress spilling into home life
- Workplace relationships becoming emotional outlets
- Ambition mismatches between partners
- Financial strain from unstable employment

Understanding these pressures allows couples to create routines that ensure the relationship remains nourished even during demanding seasons.

Setting Healthy Boundaries

Boundaries are essential for protecting emotional space and relational harmony. Without them, outside voices and situations easily drain energy from the relationship. Healthy boundaries make it clear what belongs to the couple and what belongs to the outside world. They create safety and prevent confusion, especially around loyalty, privacy, and decision-making.

Healthy boundaries often include:
- Clarifying which issues stay between partners
- Limiting family interference in marital decisions
- Agreeing on appropriate behaviour with colleagues or friends
- Managing time spent on devices and social media
- Protecting quality time from external demands

Boundaries enable couples to maintain unity, notwithstanding external pressures surrounding them.

Filtering Outside Advice

Advice comes easily—especially when people assume they understand the relationship from the outside. But well-meaning guidance can become harmful if it conflicts with the couple's values or lacks understanding of the situation. Couples must learn to evaluate advice rather than absorb it. Not every suggestion deserves attention.

Advice should be filtered by asking:
- Does this reflect our values?
- Does it strengthen our unity?
- Is the source unbiased or projecting their experience?
- Does it respect the complexity of our relationship?

When couples choose their guiding voices wisely, they strengthen their independence and clarity.

Reflection & Assessment

Personal Reflection
Who positively influences our relationship?
Who undermines or strains it?

Partner Dialogue
Where do we need clearer boundaries?

Reality Check
☐ Healthy boundaries exist

☐ External interference persists

Protecting Your Relationship

Every relationship needs a protective shield—one built through loyalty, discretion, and intentional unity. This protection is not secrecy; it is safeguarding the emotional ecosystem of the relationship. Couples protect their relationship when they refrain from exposing each other's vulnerabilities, correct false assumptions made by outsiders, and defend the dignity of their partner even in their absence.

A strong relationship is not one without external influences, but one where partners stand together—aligned, respectful, and protective of what they share.

CHAPTER 17: MARRIAGE COUNSELLING — WHEN AND HOW TO SEEK HELP

Seeking help is not a sign of failure; it is a declaration that the relationship still matters.

Counselling is a tool for understanding, growth, and healing. It is not reserved for relationships in crisis; it is a resource for any couple seeking clarity, perspective, or skills to strengthen their partnership. Yet many couples seek help too late—often when patterns have hardened, and resentment has built.

This chapter explores how counselling works, when to use it, and why it can transform relationships. The survey identifies clear warning signs. In both regions, approximately 15-16% of respondents report being unhappy in their relationships, while 20-24% would walk away if given the option. More tellingly, the gap between those who are unhappy (15%) and those who would actually leave (20-24%) suggests many couples stay together despite dissatisfaction—often waiting too long to seek help. The gap between these numbers suggests many unhappy people remain without active exit plans—a population potentially responsive to counselling intervention.

When to Seek Professional Help

Many couples wait until emotional distance becomes unbearable or conflict becomes a cycle. But counselling is most effective when challenges first begin to surface.

Common signs that counselling may help include:
- Repeating the same argument without resolution
- Feeling unheard or misunderstood
- Decrease in emotional or physical intimacy
- Avoiding difficult conversations
- Constant tension or irritability
- Trust beginning to weaken

Seeking help early preserves goodwill and prevents small misunderstandings from becoming major fractures.

Types of Counselling

Couples often encounter three types of support:

Parental or Family Counselling

This is common in traditional cultures where elders are seen as custodians of wisdom. Their advice can be comforting but is sometimes shaped by bias, emotional involvement, or generational norms.

Religious Counselling

Spiritual leaders offer guidance grounded in faith and shared values. This can help couples reconnect with spiritual principles, but it may not address psychological patterns or communication dynamics.

Professional Counselling

A trained Counsellor offers neutrality, structure, and tools. They help partners understand patterns, identify emotional triggers, improve communication, and rebuild trust. Professional counselling is often the most balanced option because it prioritises emotional safety and objectivity.

Overcoming Barriers to Seeking Help

Many people hesitate to seek counselling due to fear of judgment, cultural stigma, or the belief that couples should resolve issues privately. Men in particular may resist counselling because it challenges ideas of strength or authority. Acknowledging the need for help is a sign of maturity, not weakness. Counselling does not expose failure—it prevents it.

Preventative vs. Crisis Counselling

Preventative counselling helps couples establish patterns of healthy communication, boundary-setting, and conflict resolution before issues escalate. It works like maintenance rather than repair. Crisis counselling becomes necessary when partners feel stuck, disconnected, or distressed. While healing is still possible, the process is often slower because emotions have intensified. Couples who adopt preventative counselling earlier tend to experience fewer major conflicts later.

What to Look for in a Counsellor

A good Counsellor offers confidentiality, neutrality, and compassion. The relationship should feel safe, structured, and balanced.

Qualities of an effective Counsellor include:
- Professional training and experience
- Cultural awareness
- Ability to remain neutral
- Practical tools for communication and conflict resolution
- Respect for both partners' perspectives

Choosing the right Counsellor significantly increases the likelihood of positive outcomes.

Reflection & Assessment

Personal Reflection

What fears or assumptions have delayed seeking help?
What might change if we sought support earlier?

Partner Dialogue

How do we feel about third-party support?

Reality Check

☐ Open to counselling
☐ Resistant but curious

Making the Most of Counselling

Counselling works when both partners commit to honesty, openness, and consistent effort. It requires patience, as old patterns take time to unlearn. Couples who benefit most are those who practice the skills between sessions—improving communication, addressing conflict gently, and showing empathy even when frustrated. Counselling provides the path, but partners must walk it together.

CHAPTER 18: COMMUNICATION — THE FOUNDATION OF EVERYTHING

Communication is not about speaking more — it is about understanding deeper.

Communication is the lifeline of any relationship (See communication in Chapter 1). Without it, trust fades, intimacy weakens, and misunderstanding becomes common. Healthy communication is not simply speaking; it is connection, clarity, and emotional presence.

This chapter examines the core elements of communication that sustain long-term relationships. Across interviews, emotional withdrawal emerged as a pattern that quietly erodes connection. Partners described moments where silence replaced communication, especially during stress. This emotional distance often went unspoken, yet it shaped the quality of the relationship. A married African male in my survey said:

Well, sometimes she can be overly critical in her communication.

And another single African female said:

When he has stressful moments, he closes out on me.

Communication Styles and Differences

Differences in communication styles often come from upbringing, personality, and cultural norms. One partner may prefer direct expression, while the other communicates subtly. These differences are not flaws; they are patterns that must be understood. Couples remained loyal, yet emotionally unfulfilled, highlighting the need for tools that build understanding rather than relying on affection alone. Both regions expressed that love alone is insufficient without communication skills and emotional literacy. USA respondents prioritise personal happiness, communication, and autonomy.

Communication challenges emerge indirectly in the data. When respondents describe what they dislike about partners, American responses reveal communication themes: "Never there," "Double standards," "We don't always share the same values," and "Not enough attentiveness." African responses, while coded differently, suggest similar underlying dynamics through categories like "Other" that may encompass communication issues. Respondents frequently pointed to unmet emotional needs, lack of communication, and negative relational patterns as contributors to dissatisfaction. These quiet gaps often shape relationship experience more than external circumstances.

Common contrasting styles include:
- Direct vs. indirect expression
- Emotional vs. reserved responses
- Fast processors vs. slow processors
- Problem-solving focus vs. emotional focus

Recognising these differences helps couples respond with empathy instead of frustration.

Active Listening Skills

Many couples hear each other, but few genuinely listen. Most people listen to respond and not to understand. Active listening involves being fully present, setting aside distractions, offering empathy, and reflecting understanding.

Active listening includes:
- Allowing your partner to finish without interruption
- Validating feelings even when you disagree
- Asking clarifying questions gently
- Showing genuine interest

When partners feel heard, connection deepens immediately.

Conflict Patterns — Pursue vs. Withdraw

Most couples default to one of two patterns in conflict:
- The Pursuer, who seeks immediate discussion and resolution
- The Withdrawer, who needs time and space to process

Neither style is wrong. Conflict becomes destructive when partners interpret these differences as rejection or hostility. Understanding each other's patterns creates space for compassion.

Creating Safe Space for Difficult Conversations

Emotional safety allows partners to speak openly without fear of criticism or punishment. Conversations become safer when partners manage tone, avoid personal attacks, and choose appropriate timing. A safe environment encourages vulnerability, which is essential for intimacy.

Repairing After Communication Breakdowns

Breakdowns are inevitable. Repair is what distinguishes healthy relationships from struggling ones.

Repairing involves:
• Acknowledging hurt
• Clarifying intentions
• Apologising sincerely
• Reaffirming connection
• Agreeing on how to move forward

Couples who repair quickly prevent emotional distance from growing.

Improving Communication Effectiveness

Communication is a skill that strengthens with practice. Couples who commit to learning new habits experience fewer misunderstandings and deeper intimacy. Helpful habits include:
• Regular check-ins
• Honest expression of needs
• Managing triggers respectfully
• Avoiding assumptions
• Speaking with kindness and clarity

The quality of communication often determines the quality of the relationship.

Reflection & Assessment

Personal Reflection

Do I listen to understand or to defend?

What communication habits damage connection?

Partner Dialogue

What communication pattern hurts us most?

Reality Check (1–5)

Honesty

Respect

Emotional safety

Scan this code for a short reflection related to Part V.

PART VI - WHEN MARRIAGE ENDS AND BEGINS AGAIN

No one enters marriage planning for it to end.

We begin with hope, commitment, and the belief—spoken or silent—that this will last. For many, it does. But for many others, despite efforts, sacrifices, prayers, endurance, and years invested, marriage reaches a point where it can no longer be sustained in a healthy.

This part of the book speaks to that reality—not as failure, but as truth. Ending a marriage is one of the most emotionally complex experiences a person can face. It carries grief, guilt, relief, fear, judgment, and loss—often all at the same time. It disrupts identity, family structures, finances, social circles, and deeply held beliefs about love, commitment, and self-worth. In many cultures, including those I come from, divorce is not just a personal event; it is a communal one, often accompanied by stigma, silence, and shame.

Yet staying in a relationship that has become emotionally barren, unsafe, or fundamentally misaligned is not always noble. Sometimes, endurance becomes erosion. Sometimes, what looks like commitment from the outside is quiet self-abandonment on the inside.

This section is not written to encourage divorce. Nor is it written to romanticise it. It is written to **tell the truth**.

Marriage can end—even after decades such as mine. And when it does, life does not end with it.

Divorce is not the opposite of love. In many cases, it is the consequence of love that was never properly understood, nurtured, or aligned. It can also be the beginning of deeper self-awareness, emotional healing, and—eventually—a healthier form of companionship.

In this part, we will explore:

How to emotionally process the end of a marriage

How to navigate grief, identity loss, and societal judgment

How to heal without rushing or hardening

How to recognise patterns that should not be repeated

And how, when the time is right, love can be approached again—more consciously, more honestly, and more wisely

An ending can also be a bridge.

A bridge between who you were and who you are becoming. A bridge between survival and peace. A bridge between repeating the past and choosing differently.

If you are reading this section while still married, my hope is that it helps you make conscious choices—whether that means rebuilding with clarity or releasing with dignity. If you are reading this after a divorce, I hope it offers reassurance that healing is possible and that your story is not over. And if you are considering love again, I hope these chapters help you cross into it with wisdom rather than fear.

Marriage may end. But life, growth, and love can begin again.

This is not the end of the journey. For many like me, it is the most honest beginning.

CHAPTER 19: DIVORCE, HEALING AND SECOND CHANCES

An ending can break you, or it can rebuild you — the difference is reflection.

This is the hardest chapter for me to write. It's also one of the most important. My story isn't just about divorce. It's about the years of pain that preceded it, the courage it took to finally act, the healing that followed, and the joy of discovering that second chances are real. If you're considering divorce, going through one, or recovering from one, this chapter is for you. I'll share what I learned through failure, pain, and eventual healing—not to tell you what to do, but to help you make the best decision for your situation with full awareness of what lies ahead.

Divorce is often spoken about in our society and where it is discussed, it is stigmatised. It will shock you to know that according to the latest *Marriages and Divorces* statistical release from **Statistics South Africa (Stats SA),** a total of **22,230 divorces were finalised in 2023,** reflecting a **10.1% increase from the 20,196 divorces recorded in 2022.**

The **Centers for Disease Control and Prevention (CDC), National Center for Health Statistics (2023)** reported that the US national divorce rate stood at **2.4 divorces per 1,000 population,** based on provisional data from reporting states. What is particularly sobering is that **42% of these marriages ended within the first ten years,** and **55.1% involved couples with children under the age of eighteen.**

These exclude unreported divorce cases. Therefore, divorce must be approached not merely as a personal failure, but as a complex human transition—one that requires emotional honesty, accountability, and healing. Understanding this does not normalise divorce, nor does it trivialise its consequences. Instead, it removes the illusion that "it only happens to others."

The Truth About My First Marriage

This is my truth about what went wrong and my ex-wife might have a different view. As discussed in the Introduction Chapter, let me be honest about something that's painful to admit: My first marriage lacked the *Three pillars* (See Chapter 3), but I didn't realize it—or wouldn't admit it—for decades. Attempts at intervention—from friends, relatives, and spiritual leaders to resolve our differences did not help, largely because they were viewed as lacking objectivity.

Some of the factors that contributed to the failure of my first marriage included:

Lack of understanding and empathy

Because we didn't truly know each other very well before marriage, we entered it as strangers. We spent decades trying to understand ourselves, something that should have happened before committing.

Different values and priorities

We wanted different things from life, had different approaches to money, and different ideas about how to live. These weren't small differences—they were fundamental incompatibilities we couldn't bridge.

Communication breakdown

The difference in our education levels created a communication barrier from day one. We couldn't discuss ideas, couldn't share intellectual interests, couldn't connect at that level. This gap only widened over the years. This on its own would not have been a problem if there was growth mindset.

Towards the end, we could barely talk and actively avoided each other because seeing each other triggered anxiety for both of us. Even simple conversations were difficult.

Mutual unhappiness

This wasn't about one person being the villain and the other the victim. We were both miserable. The marriage wasn't working for either of us, as she said to me at one time that having conversations with me gave her anxiety.

The painful truth: There was no genuine connection from the beginning. We were young, inexperienced, following society, religious and cultural expectations, and didn't know any better.

The Decision-Making Process

Making the final decision to divorce required brutal honesty with myself:

Question 1: Have I genuinely tried everything?

Yes. I'd tried counselling multiple times. I'd sought spiritual guidance. I'd worked on myself. I'd tried to change my expectations. There was nothing left to try.

Question 2: Is there any realistic chance this marriage will improve?

No. Decades of patterns don't suddenly change. We'd proven over nearly four decades that we couldn't make it work. Hoping for change at this point was delusional.

Question 3: What am I sacrificing by staying?

My happiness. My mental health. My remaining years. The chance to experience genuine companionship and love. The possibility of modelling a healthy relationship for my children.

Question 4: What is my wife sacrificing by staying?

The same things in my view. She was as unhappy as I was. She deserved the chance to find happiness too, even though she wasn't the one initiating the divorce.

Question 5: Are my children genuinely benefiting from our staying together?

No. They were adults. They'd told us during the divorce process that their concern was our happiness. They didn't need us to remain in an unhappy marriage for their sake. They needed us to be healthy, fulfilled people. Speaking for myself, I was not happy.

Question 6: What am I teaching my children by staying in an unhappy marriage?

That suffering silently is virtue. That you should sacrifice your wellbeing for others' approval. That marriage means tolerating unhappiness. These weren't lessons I wanted to teach.

Literary accounts such as Buch Emecheta's portrayal of endurance and emotional silence in marriage echo the reality that, staying can coexist with deep loneliness, and that endurance is not always synonymous with relational health (Emecheta, 1979).

Question 7: Is there any moral or practical reason to stay?

At this point, children grown up, every intervention tried—no. The only thing keeping me was the fear of the unknown, societal judgement and inertia.

Question 8: If I died tomorrow, would I regret not having taken this step?

Yes. Absolutely. I would regret wasting my final years in misery when I could have pursued happiness. That last question clarified everything.

Telling The Children

After I decided to move on, I realised I had to inform our children, so I set up a meeting with all four of them. Their mother was present. I'd prepared what I wanted to say. I told them:

- I had filed for divorce
- This was my decision, not their mother's
- We had both tried for many years to make it work
- We were both unhappy
- I believed divorce was better for both of us
- They were not responsible for this
- We both loved them
- We would both remain their parents

Their response was: "As long as you're both happy" which implied they probably knew all along we were unhappy. All my attempts to hide it, to stay together "for the sake of the children"—they'd seen through it. Children always do.

Impact of The Divorce Process:

Relief mixed with grief

Even when you're leaving an unhappy marriage, there's grief. Grief for the dreams you had, for the years invested, for the life you thought you'd have. Grief for what never was, not just what ended.

Practical complications

Emotional roller-coaster, uncertain future, fear of starting all over again without a guarantee of happiness.

Social navigation

Telling friends, family, colleagues. Managing others' reactions—surprise, judgment, pity, unsolicited advice. In Africa where I lived, divorce still carries a stigma.

Emotional exhaustion

Even when divorce is the right decision, the process is emotionally draining. There were days I questioned everything. Days I felt guilty, selfish, frightened. But also hope: For the first time in years, I felt hope. Hope that life could be different. Hope that happiness was possible. Hope that we could both find genuine companionship.

Aftermath:

The year following finalization was healing time. I focused on:

- Processing what had happened
- Understanding my own mistakes and patterns
- Determining what I actually needed in a relationship
- Building a life as a single person
- Reconnecting with myself after years of disconnection

This wasn't easy. Who was I without this marriage? What did I want? What kind of person did I want to become?

The Turning Point: Writing This Book

During my healing year, I revisited the book on relationships I had been writing for years, compiling what would become this book. I reflected on everything I'd learned—from my childhood in a polygamous household, from my marriage, from my divorce, from observing countless couples through my survey research.

The eight factors to consider in choosing a partner (Chapter 4)? I'd ignored most of them when I married at 25. The importance of courtship for truly knowing each other (Chapter 5)? We'd barely had one. Communication as the foundation (Chapter 18)? We'd never been able to communicate effectively. Financial compatibility (Chapter 9)? We'd struggled with it throughout. Sustaining relationships through intentional investment (Chapter 8)? We'd never built that foundation. Everything I'd written in this book—all the advice, all the research, all the principles—I'd violated in my first marriage.

Had I had followed my own advice—the advice I'm giving you in this book—my first marriage either would never have happened, or it would have been healthier. Writing this book clarified what I needed to do differently next time.

My Second Marriage

A second marriage is not a continuation of the first; it is a new creation shaped by experience, clarity, and emotional maturity. Individuals who remarry after divorce often do so with deeper self-awareness and a clearer understanding of the qualities needed for a healthy partnership. My journey into a second marriage began only after I had taken time to heal, reflect, and regain clarity about the kind of relationship I desired. I knew that if I wanted a different outcome, I needed to enter the next relationship with intention and emotional honesty.

Healing was essential. I needed to ensure that old wounds would not shape a new relationship. I took my time looking for the right person, making sure I did not repeat the mistakes of the past. This allowed me to approach new love with stability rather than fear, and with clarity rather than confusion. The healing process also helped me identify my non-negotiables: emotional safety, open communication, mutual respect, intellectual compatibility, and shared responsibility.

Clarity became my strongest tool. By the time I met my current wife, I had already completed parts of this book. I had articulated for myself the qualities that matter most in a partner and the behaviours that sustain a marriage. As I reflect on that period, I see how much this clarity helped me choose wisely. I knew what I was looking for, and I recognised it when I saw it. Decisions that once felt complicated became straightforward because I now understood my values, needs, and relational patterns.

When two people meet at the right stage of emotional readiness, time becomes less relevant than alignment. One of the most important decisions I made before remarrying was to go through marriage coaching. Coaching gave us the tools to understand our communication patterns, manage conflict, and align expectations. It also allowed us to discuss our pasts openly and build a foundation based on mutual awareness.

My second marriage is built on companionship, mutual understanding, and emotional freedom. We enjoy spending time together, communicate openly, and notice each other's emotional signals. This mutual awareness has reduced conflict and increased connection.

We frequently affirm one another, go for walks, and share some quiet moments together. These small but meaningful habits have become the core of our relationship. Peace, not perfection, defines this second chapter of my life. What I have now is not the product of luck — it is the result of growth, clarity, and intentionality.

Today, I live in a partnership where communication is natural, companionship is genuine, and peace is constant. We reaffirm each other daily. We express appreciation, acknowledge efforts, and celebrate each other. When we disagree (rarely), we resolve it through communication and respect. No yelling, no silent treatment, no avoidance.

I know now, with confidence, that I am happy — and that happiness was made possible by healing the past and choosing differently for the future.

The Bottom Line

This is what marriage should be. This is companionship, partnership, and love. This is what I wish I'd had from the beginning.

What My Story Teaches About Divorce

Marriages rarely collapse overnight. They unravel slowly through silence, distance, and unmet emotional needs. Our relationships deteriorated over time to the point where we started avoiding one another to avoid tension. Eventually, I realised that seeing each other triggered anxiety for both of us, and living together became extremely difficult.

When a home no longer provides emotional safety, the marriage is already a source of stress. Research shows that persistent emotional tension is more damaging to adults — and to children — than respectful separation.

My decision to finally proceed with divorce came after I was confronted with the reality of spending the rest of my life in a relationship that brought neither joy nor peace. This clarity was painful, but it became the catalyst for change.

Rebuilding requires honest evaluation of past patterns. These reflections are not about assigning blame but about understanding the structural weaknesses that made the marriage unsustainable. Clarity about what went wrong becomes the foundation on which healthier future relationships are built.

Life after divorce requires re-learning about oneself. I gradually rediscovered emotional quiet, personal hobbies, and the ability to make independent decisions without the constant weight of marital tension. This period became a time of growth and preparation for the possibility of companionship built on better foundations. Rebuilding after divorce is not about replacing someone. It is about rediscovering who you are — and who you can become.

Let me extract the lessons from my experience:

Lesson 1: Choose Wisely

This is the most important lesson. If I'd been more careful in my choice, if I'd paid attention to compatibility factors, if I'd not just followed cultural and religious expectations—I could have avoided the years of unhappiness and a painful divorce. Prevention is infinitely easier than repair. No just this chapter, everything in this book up to this point is meant to assist you in choosing wisely from the beginning.

Lesson 2: "Staying for the Children" Is More Complicated Than It Seems

I told myself for years that I was staying for my children's sake. The truth? My children were fine with the divorce. They wanted us to be happy. They'd rather have two happy separated parents than two miserable married ones. Now, timing matters—divorcing when children are very young creates different challenges than divorcing when they're adults. But don't assume your children need you to stay in an unhappy marriage. Sometimes the healthiest thing you can model for them is knowing when to leave.

Lesson 3: Empathy for Your Spouse Can Keep You Trapped

My empathy for my ex-wife—my concern for her well-being, her financial security, her social standing—partly kept me in an unhappy marriage for years. This empathy was good in one sense (I wasn't a cruel person), but it prevented me from seeing that she was also unhappy. She deserved better too. My staying wasn't helping her either. Sometimes the most empathetic thing you can do is end a marriage that's not working for either of you.

Lesson 4: Multiple Divorce Filings Signal Deep Problems

I filed for divorce four times over a period of nineteen years. That wasn't normal cold feet—that was my intuition screaming at me that this marriage wasn't working, while my obligations and fears kept pulling me back. If you're repeatedly considering divorce, that's not a small problem. That's your soul telling you something needs to change—either the marriage needs serious intervention, or it needs to end.

Lesson 5: Healing Takes Time, But It Happens

I needed time to heal after the divorce. That years of being single, processing, understanding myself was essential. I couldn't have jumped immediately into a new relationship healthily. Time heals. Give yourself the permission to take that time.

Lesson 6: Second Chances Are Real

I found genuine love and companionship after the divorce. Second chances happen. Happiness after divorce is possible. You are not doomed to be alone or miserable forever.

Lesson 7: Learning From Failure Creates Success

My first marriage taught me what not to do. My divorce taught me what I actually needed. Writing this book helped me clarify principles I'd violated. All of that failure prepared me for success in my second marriage. Failure isn't final—it's educational if you let it be.

What to Know About Divorce

Common Reasons for Divorce:
- Communication breakdown
- Financial conflicts

- Infidelity
- Incompatibility that couldn't be resolved
- Loss of love/respect
- Abuse (physical or emotional)

Factors That Made Divorce Harder:
- Children (especially young children)
- Financial dependence
- Religious beliefs against divorce
- Cultural stigma
- Fear of being alone
- Fear of hurting spouse

What Helped People Through Divorce:
- Professional counselling
- Support from friends/family
- Time and patience with healing
- Focusing on children's wellbeing (for those with kids)
- Building a new identity as a single person
- Eventually finding a new relationship

When Divorce Is Necessary

Not all marriages should be saved. Sometimes divorce is the healthiest option for everyone involved.

Divorce may be necessary when:

1. There's Abuse

Physical, emotional, sexual, or financial abuse. If you're being harmed, your safety is more important than preserving the marriage.

2. There's Unrepentant Infidelity

If your spouse cheats, shows no remorse, continues the affair, or serially cheats—the relationship is already broken. You're just acknowledging it.

3. There's Active Addiction That's Unaddressed

If your spouse is addicted (alcohol, drugs, gambling, etc.) and refuses treatment or repeatedly relapses—you can't force them to change. Sometimes you have to save yourself.

4. You've Genuinely Tried Everything

If you've tried counselling, intervention, changed yourself, given it years, exhausted all options—and nothing changes—divorce may be the only option left.

5. You're Fundamentally Incompatible

Sometimes two people are just wrong for each other. Not abusive, not evil—just incompatible in ways that can't be bridged. My first marriage was this.

6. The Marriage Harms Your Mental/Physical Health

If staying is destroying your health, sanity, or well-being, your life matters more than the marriage.

7. Both Parties Are Miserable

Sometimes letting go of each other is the most considerate thing to do if neither party is pleased and no amount of work can change that.

When To Try Harder Before Divorcing

Not all troubled marriages should end. Sometimes divorce is premature.

Try harder if:

1. You Haven't Truly Tried

If you've never done serious counselling, never really worked on yourself, never addressed the issues—try first before giving up.

2. You're in a Stressful Season That Will Pass

New baby, job loss, health crisis, family emergency—extreme stress affects all marriages. Don't make permanent decisions during temporary crises.

3. There's Still Love and Respect

If you still love each other, still respect each other, still want to make it work—you have a foundation to build on. Get help and keep trying.

4. You're Running From Yourself, Not the Marriage

Sometimes the problem isn't your spouse—it's you. Your unresolved trauma, your unrealistic expectations, your unwillingness to compromise. Don't divorce to escape yourself; you'll carry those issues to the next relationship.

5. Your Children Are Very Young

This is complicated, but if possible, give it more time and more effort when children are very young. They need stability. (But if there's abuse or severe harm, leave regardless.)

6. You Haven't Addressed Specific, Fixable Problems

If your marriage has clear problems that haven't been addressed—money management, communication skills, unresolved past issues—try addressing them specifically first.

7. You're Making the Decision From Fear or Pressure

Don't divorce because you're scared or because others are pressuring you. Make this decision from clarity and conviction.

How To Decide

If you're considering divorce, here's a framework:

Step 1: Get Individual Counselling

Before deciding, work with a therapist individually and together. Understand your own motivations, patterns, and unresolved issues. Sometimes what feels like marital problems are individual issues you're projecting onto your spouse.

Step 2: Insist on Couples Counselling

If your spouse won't go to counselling to save the marriage, that tells you something about their commitment. If they are willing to go, give it genuine effort.

Step 3: Create Separation if Needed

Sometimes a trial separation clarifies things. Living apart temporarily (with clear parameters and a timeline) helps you understand whether you want to repair or end the marriage.

Step 4: Ask the Hard Questions

- Have we genuinely tried everything?
- Is there a. realistic possibility this will improve?
- What am I sacrificing by staying?
- What am I gaining by leaving?
- Are my children better served by us staying together or divorcing?
- What am I teaching my children about relationships and self-respect?
- Am I making this decision from fear or from wisdom?
- If I died tomorrow, would I regret this decision?

Step 5: Give it Time, Then Act

Don't make impulsive decisions. But also, don't let indecision become a decision by default. Set a timeline. If nothing changes by then, act. I filed for divorce four times over nineteen years because I kept hoping things would change. They never did. I should have either committed to staying and making the best of it, or left decisively. The limbo was torture for both of us.

The Divorce Process: Practical Realities

If you decide to divorce, here's what to expect:

Legal Process:

- Find a good divorce attorney
- Understand your jurisdiction's laws
- Prepare for financial disclosure
- Negotiate division of assets
- Establish custody arrangements (if you have children)
- Expect it to take months (sometimes years)

Financial Impact:

- Costs money (attorney fees, court costs)
- Division of assets and debts
- Possible alimony or child support
- Establishing separate households
- Rebuilding separate financial lives

Emotional Impact:
- Grief (even when it's the right decision)
- Anger, guilt, fear, sadness
- Loss of identity as a married person
- Loneliness
- Relief mixed with mourning
- Processing failure

Social Impact:
- Telling people (which is harder than expected)
- Managing others' reactions
- Possible judgment or stigma
- Changes in friendships (some friends take sides)
- Navigating social events as a single person
- Dealing with unsolicited advice

Practical Impact:
- Moving/new living arrangements
- New daily routines
- Learning to be alone
- Rebuilding social life
- Managing co-parenting (if applicable)

What Helps:
- Professional counselling
- Supportive friends/family
- Taking care of physical health
- Maintaining routines
- Focusing on children's needs
- Giving yourself grace
- Time and patience

Healing After Divorce

Healing doesn't happen overnight. Here's what the process looked like for me:

Immediate Phase (0-3 Months):
- Relief mixed with grief
- Practical adjustments to single life

- Telling people, managing reactions
- Establishing new routines
- Processing what happened

Early Healing Phase (3-12 Months):
- Deeper grief work
- Understanding my own role in marital failure
- Identifying patterns to avoid repeating
- Rebuilding identity as a single person
- Beginning to feel hopeful

Later Healing Phase (12-24 Months):
- Accepting what happened
- Forgiving myself and my ex-wife
- Feeling whole as a single person
- Open to new relationships
- Clarity about what I need

Keys to Healing:
- Don't rush
- Process your emotions (counselling helps)
- Take responsibility for your part
- Forgive (doesn't mean reconciling, means releasing bitterness)
- Learn from the experience
- Build a new life before seeking new relationship
- Know you're ready before dating

Advice For Those Considering Divorce

If you're thinking about divorce:

Don't:
- Make impulsive decisions
- Divorce without trying counselling first
- Use divorce as a threat during arguments
- Rush into a decision due to temporary frustration
- Make your spouse the villain and yourself the victim
- Involve children in adult decisions
- Badmouth your spouse to others
- Make decisions based on others' expectations

Do:
- Get individual counselling first
- Try couples counselling seriously
- Take time to make the decision
- Consider all factors (children, finances, etc.)
- Be honest with yourself about your role
- Seek wise Counsel from people who know you both

- Think long-term, not just about current pain
- Make a decision based on your reality, not fear

Remember:
- Divorce is painful even when necessary
- Your children will be affected (but can be okay)
- Healing is possible
- Second chances exist
- You will survive this
- The decision is ultimately yours

Advice For Those Going Through Divorce

If you're in the middle of a divorce:

Priorities:
1. Your emotional/mental health
2. Your children's well-being (if applicable)
3. Fair legal/financial settlement
4. Maintaining dignity and integrity
5. Beginning the healing process

Don't:
- Use children as weapons
- Try to destroy your ex
- Make it messier than necessary
- Post about it constantly on social media
- Date before you're healed
- Isolate yourself completely
- Ignore your mental health

Do:
- Get good legal Counsel
- Protect your children from conflict
- Take care of your health
- Build a support system
- Allow yourself to grieve
- Set boundaries with your ex
- Focus on what you can control
- Look forward, not just backward

Remember:
- This is temporary even though it feels endless
- You're stronger than you think
- Help is available
- Your children need you to be healthy

- This doesn't define you forever
- Better days are coming

Advice For Those Healing After Divorce

If your divorce is finalized and you're rebuilding:

Focus on:
- Understanding what happened and your role
- Processing grief and loss
- Forgiving yourself and your ex
- Building a new identity and life
- Reconnecting with yourself
- Determining what you need if/when you date again
- Being whole as a single person before seeking a relationship

Don't:
- Rush into a new relationship
- Seek a relationship to fill the void
- Bring unhealed baggage to a new partner
- Repeat the same patterns
- Stay bitter forever
- Define yourself by divorce
- Give up on love

Do:
- Take all the time you need
- Therapy is valuable
- Rebuild self-esteem
- Create a new life you enjoy
- Reconnect with friends and interests
- Eventually be open to love again
- Know you're ready before dating
- Do it differently next time

Remember:
- Healing isn't linear
- You will have good and bad days
- Time genuinely helps
- You can be happy again
- Second chances are real
- You deserve love and companionship
- Your story isn't over

The Gift of My Failed First Marriage

Here's something counterintuitive: I'm grateful for my first marriage—not despite its failure, but because of what it taught me.

That marriage taught me:
• What I actually need in a partner
• The importance of compatibility across all dimensions
• That love alone isn't enough—you need communication, respect, shared values
• The cost of ignoring warning signs and cultural pressure
• The pain of spending decades with someone you don't connect with.
• The courage it takes to admit failure and start over
• That second chances are possible
• Everything I needed to know to get it right the second time

Without that failed marriage, I wouldn't have written this book. I wouldn't have done the research. I wouldn't have understood relationship dynamics so deeply. I wouldn't have known what to look for in my second marriage. My failure became my education. And now I'm sharing that education with you so you don't have to learn these lessons the same painful way I did.

To Those Facing This Decision

If you're reading this chapter because you're considering divorce, let me speak directly to you: This is one of the hardest decisions you'll ever make. There's no easy answer. There's no path without pain. But staying in a marriage that's destroying you isn't noble—it's tragic. Your life matters. Your happiness matters. Your mental health matters.

Healing does not begin with the legal dissolution; it begins with acceptance. For me, recovery required time, reflection, and emotional recalibration. Time truly does heal wounds when it is used intentionally — not to suppress pain, but to understand it.

During the healing process, I reconnected with aspects of myself that had been overshadowed by years of marital strain. I had to rebuild my identity beyond the role of husband and father. I needed to rediscover what brought me peace, what I valued, and how I wanted to live the next chapter of my life.

Your children need you healthy more than they need you married.

Model self-respect, healthy boundaries, and the courage to make hard decisions. Don't model martyrdom and misery. If you've genuinely tried everything and nothing changes, it's okay to leave. You're not a failure. You're not selfish. You're human. Take your time with this decision. Don't rush. But also, don't let fear of deciding keep you in limbo for decades like I did.

Get help making this decision. Professional counselling. Wise mentors. People who know you and your situation. Whatever you decide, commit to it. If you stay, really stay—stop considering divorce and work on making the best marriage possible. If you leave, really leave—do it with as much dignity and integrity as possible. And know this: If you do divorce, healing is possible. Happiness is possible. Second chances are real. You are not doomed. You will survive this. Life can be good again. I'm a living proof of that.

Reflection & Assessment

Personal Reflection
>What lessons must I carry forward?
>What patterns must I consciously release?

Reality Check
>☐ Healing in progress
>☐ Healing avoided

The Bottom Line

Divorce isn't failure—sometimes it's necessary growth. Sometimes staying is the failure—failure to respect yourself, failure to acknowledge reality, failure to model healthy relationships for your children.

I stayed years in a marriage that didn't serve any of us. Was that noble? Or was it wasted time for both of us? I don't know the answer to that. What I do know:

- The pain was real
- The divorce was painful but necessary
- Healing happened
- Second chances are real
- I'm genuinely happy now
- Both of us deserved better
- Our children are fine
- Life goes on

If I could do it over, I would have followed all the advice in this book. But since I can't redo the past, I can only learn from it and share those lessons with you. If you're before marriage: Choose wisely. Follow the guidance in this book. Don't ignore compatibility factors. Don't rush. Don't just follow cultural expectations. Your choice of partner is the most important decision you'll ever make.

If you're in a struggling marriage: Get help. Try everything. But also know when enough is enough. Don't waste decades in misery out of guilt or fear.

If you're divorced or considering it: You're not alone. Healing is possible. You can be happy again. Second chances are real. If I can find it after divorce, you can too. Don't give up. Don't stay trapped. Make the best decision for your unique situation with all the wisdom, support, and courage you can muster.

And remember: Your story isn't over. The next chapter might be the best one yet.

PART VII - THE LONG VIEW: AGING TOGETHER & LEGACY

The survey's most hopeful finding emerges from age-stratified analysis. Among USA respondents aged 65 and older, satisfaction reaches 100%—both happiness and trust. While this could reflect survivor bias (unhappy couples having already divorced), it more likely indicates that couples who persist through the challenging middle years find their greatest rewards in later life.

The middle years prove most challenging. Respondents aged 35-44 show the lowest satisfaction rates in both cultures, likely reflecting the stress of peak career demands combined with active child-rearing. This mid-life relationship dip appears universal, suggesting that couples should prepare for this challenging period and take comfort that satisfaction typically rebounds.

Legacy manifests in how respondents describe their partners' best qualities. African responses emphasize character virtues: "Honesty and pure love," "Humility, integrity, upbringing or values," "He is my best friend... the friendship will always last even when everything else is not there." These descriptions suggest that lasting relationships build legacies of character that outlive passion.

The widowed respondents—1% of the African sample and 3% of American—provide poignant data points. All widowed respondents who answered happiness questions reported being happy with their (now-ended) relationships, and none indicated they would have walked away. This suggests that relationships ended by death rather than choice often leave positive legacies.

CHAPTER 20: OLD AGE AND RELATIONSHIPS

A lasting marriage is not measured by years survived, but by intimacy sustained.

Growing Older Together.

At my age, I'm living what many of you are preparing for: the later years of life and marriage. My second marriage is young, but I have perspective from decades of experience, from watching my parents age, and from observing countless elderly couples. This chapter addresses the realities of aging in marriage—the challenges, adjustments, joys, and preparations you should make now for the decades ahead.

The Reality of Aging Together

Let me start with honesty: Aging changes everything. Your body changes. Your circumstances change. Your needs change. Your relationship must adapt or it will fail.

The Stages of Aging In Marriage

Stage 1: Early Retirement (60-70)

This is where I am now. The children are launched. Work is ending or has ended. You're entering a new phase.

The Challenges:
- Adjusting to being together all the time (if both retired)
- Loss of work identity and purpose
- Financial adjustments to fixed income
- Determining how to spend increased time together
- Navigating if one retires before the other
- Health issues beginning to emerge

The Opportunities:
- Freedom to travel and pursue interests
- Time to deepen your relationship
- Reconnecting after busy work/parenting years
- Pursuing postponed dreams together
- Building legacy through grandchildren, mentoring, and service

Stage 2: Active Senior Years (70-80)

Still relatively healthy and active, but aging is more evident.

The Challenges:
- Increasing health concerns
- Friends and family members dying
- Reduced physical capabilities
- Memory changes
- Adjustment to being "elderly,"
- Possible need to stop driving
- Considering when to downsize the home

The Opportunities:
- Deep companionship built over decades
- Wisdom to handle challenges calmly
- Appreciation for every day together
- Time with grandchildren and great-grandchildren
- Leaving a legacy through relationships and wisdom

Stage 3: Declining Years (80+)

Serious health issues become more common. Independence may be challenged.

The Challenges:
- Significant health problems
- Possible need for caregiving
- Loss of independence
- Cognitive decline possibilities
- Difficult decisions about living arrangements
- One spouse may predecease the other
- Preparing for end of life

The Opportunities:
- Showing love through caregiving
- Honouring commitment "in sickness and health."
- Family support and gratitude
- Peaceful acceptance of mortality
- Knowing you've lived and loved well

Retirement: The Marriage Test

Retirement significantly impacts marriages. After decades of work, structuring your time and identity, suddenly you're together constantly.

Why Retirement Strains Some Marriages:

Challenge 1: Too Much Togetherness

You've spent 40 years with separate work lives, separate routines, separate identities. Suddenly, you're together 24/7. This can feel suffocating.

Solution: Maintain some separate activities, interests, and friendships. Togetherness is good; constant togetherness can be overwhelming. It's okay to have "alone time" or pursue individual interests.

Challenge 2: Different Retirement Visions

One partner wants to travel constantly; the other wants to stay home. One wants adventure; the other wants peace. These differences create conflict.

Solution: Discuss retirement vision before it arrives. Compromise. Maybe you travel some, stay home some. Maybe you do some activities together, some apart.

Challenge 3: Loss of Purpose

Work provided identity, purpose, and structure. Without it, some people feel lost, leading to depression, irritability, or unhealthy coping.

Solution: Develop a new purpose before retiring. Volunteer work, hobbies, mentoring, part-time work, and grandparenting. Purpose matters at every age.

Challenge 4: Financial Stress

Fixed income, rising costs, and medical expenses—financial stress can reignite old money conflicts.

Solution: Plan financially well before retirement. Work with a financial advisor. Budget realistically. Adjust lifestyle to match retirement income.

Challenge 5: One Retires Before the Other

When one spouse retires, and the other continues working, resentment can build.

Solution: Discuss expectations clearly. The retired spouse shouldn't demand the working spouse's time or resent their continued work. The working spouse shouldn't expect the retired spouse to do all household tasks.

What Makes Retirement Good for Marriage:
- Time to reconnect after busy years
- Freedom to pursue shared interests
- Travel and new experiences
- Pursuing postponed dreams
- Serving together
- Simply enjoying each other's company

Health Challenges in Aging Marriages

Health issues are inevitable in aging. How you handle them determines the quality of your marriage quality in later years.

Common Health Challenges:

Physical Health:
- Chronic conditions (diabetes, heart disease, arthritis)
- Cancer
- Mobility issues
- Chronic pain
- Reduced energy and stamina
- Sexual function changes
- Need for medications with side effects

Mental Health:
- Depression (especially in men post-retirement)
- Anxiety
- Cognitive decline or dementia
- Adjustment disorders

Sensory Changes:
- Hearing loss
- Vision problems
- These affect communication and intimacy

How Health Issues Affect Marriage:

Changed dynamics: The healthy spouse becomes caregiver. The dynamic shifts from partners to caregiver/patient. This changes the relationship fundamentally.

Sexual intimacy changes: Health issues, medications, and reduced energy all affect sexual intimacy. Couples must adapt or this becomes a source of frustration.

Communication challenges: Hearing loss makes communication difficult. Cognitive decline changes the person you married.

Emotional strain: Watching your spouse suffer is painful. Being the sick one creates guilt about burdening your spouse.

Financial impact: Medical costs, even with insurance, can devastate retirement savings.

Social isolation: Health limitations may reduce social activities, increasing isolation.

Role reversal: If the traditionally strong spouse becomes dependent, both must adjust to role reversal.

Navigating Health Challenges:

Strategy 1: Address Health Issues Promptly

Don't ignore symptoms. Don't delay seeking help. Early intervention often prevents worse problems.

Strategy 2: Both Partners Attend Medical Appointments

The healthy spouse should attend appointments to:

* Understand the diagnosis and treatment
* Ask questions the patient might forget
* Provide accurate medical history
* Support decision-making

Strategy 3: Adapt Intimacy

Sexual intimacy may need to change, but intimacy itself remains crucial. Non-sexual physical affection becomes even more important:

* Holding hands
* Gentle touches
* Sitting close
* Massage
* Cuddling

These maintain connection when sex becomes difficult or impossible.

Strategy 4: Maintain Communication

If hearing loss is an issue:

* Face each other when talking
* Speak clearly (not necessarily louder)
* Reduce background noise
* Consider hearing aids
* Use touch to get attention before speaking
* Be patient with repetition

Strategy 5: Share Caregiving Burden

If one spouse needs significant care:

* Accept help from family, friends, professionals
* Use respite care to give caregiver breaks
* Join caregiver support groups
* Don't try to do everything alone
* Remember: You can't care for someone else if you're depleted

Strategy 6: Discuss Difficult Topics

Before you're in crisis, discuss:

* What level of care are you comfortable providing at home?
* When would a nursing facility become necessary?
* What are your wishes if you become incapacitated?
* Who makes medical decisions if you can't?
* What end-of-life care do you want?

These conversations are uncomfortable but essential.

Strategy 7: Find Joy Despite Illness

Don't let illness consume everything. Find moments of joy, laughter, and beauty. Watch sunsets. Listen to music. Share memories. Appreciate what you still have.

Cognitive Decline And Dementia

This deserves special attention because it fundamentally changes the person you married.

The Unique Pain of Dementia:

Unlike physical illness, dementia changes personality, memories, and recognition. You're caring for someone who may not remember you, may not be the person you married.

Supporting Spouses Through Dementia:

• Treasure the moments of lucidity when they occur

• Remember who they were, not just who they are now

• Don't take angry or hurtful words personally (it's the disease)

• Connect with them emotionally, even when cognitive connection is gone

• Use music, photos, and familiar routines to soothe

• Get support—caregiver groups, respite care, counselling

• Know when care exceeds what you can provide at home

• Don't feel guilty if facility care becomes necessary

• Visit regularly, even if they don't recognize you

The Changed Sexual Landscape

Let's address what many books avoid: Sex changes as you age. For some couples, this is relief. For others, it's a loss.

How Aging Affects Sexual Intimacy:

Physical changes:

• Men: Erectile function may decline, need more stimulation, longer refractory period

• Women: Vaginal dryness (treatable), reduced sensitivity, pain possible

• Both: Less energy, more health issues affecting desire/ability

• Medications affecting sexual function

Emotional factors:

• Body image changes (less attractive in your own eyes)

• Lifelong patterns of unsatisfying sex become harder to change

• Shame about aging bodies

• Assumptions that "old people don't have sex"

Adapting Sexual Intimacy:

Option 1: Continue with Adaptations

Many couples maintain sexual intimacy with adjustments:

- More time for arousal
- Different positions accommodating physical limitations
- Use of lubricants
- Medical interventions (medications, devices)
- Focus on pleasure rather than performance
- Broader definition of "sex" beyond intercourse

Option 2: Transition to Non-Sexual Intimacy

Some couples naturally or by necessity transition away from sex while maintaining an intimate connection:

- Daily affectionate touch
- Cuddling and holding
- Massage
- Sleeping close
- Romantic gestures
- Verbal affection

Option 3: Acceptance of Changed Reality

Some couples accept that sexual intimacy has ended, and that's okay if both partners are at peace with it. What's NOT okay: One partner desperately wants physical intimacy while the other dismisses or refuses. This requires honest conversation and compromise.

Preparing for End of Life

Nobody wants to think about death, but preparation shows love and reduces suffering.

Essential Conversations:

Medical Wishes:

- Do you want aggressive medical intervention or comfort care?
- What life-sustaining measures do you want (or not want)?
- Where do you want to die (home, hospice, hospital)?
- Pain management priorities
- Organ donation wishes

Legal Documents:

- Will (updated regularly)
- Power of Attorney for healthcare
- Power of Attorney for finances
- Living Will/Advanced Directive
- Funeral/burial instructions

Practical Information:

- Location of important documents
- Account information and passwords

- Insurance policies
- Debts and obligations
- People to notify

Emotional Preparation:
- What you want said at your funeral
- Messages for family members
- Forgiveness you want to seek or give
- How you want to be remembered
- Appreciation you want expressed

Widowhood: The Final Chapter for Many Marriages

Most marriages end not in divorce but in death. One of you will likely face widowhood.

The Reality of Losing Your Spouse:

Widowhood is profound grief. You've lost your partner, your companion, your best friend, the person who knew you best. You're navigating life alone after decades of partnership.

What Helps Widows/Widowers:

Immediately:
- Support from family and friends
- Help with funeral arrangements
- Practical assistance (meals, household tasks)
- Space to grieve
- Not being alone constantly

Early Months:
- Grief counselling or support groups
- Maintaining routines
- Staying connected to people
- Not making major decisions immediately
- Allowing yourself to grieve

Long Term:
- Rebuilding identity as a single person
- Finding new purpose
- Staying socially connected
- Eventually being open to companionship (if desired)
- Honouring your spouse's memory while living your life

Making The Most of Your Later Years

Rather than just surviving aging, how do you thrive?

Strategy 1: Treasure Every Day

At our age, we know time is limited. Don't waste it on petty conflicts, grudges, or meaningless pursuits. Focus on what matters—love, family, contribution, joy.

Strategy 2: Express Appreciation Regularly

Don't assume your spouse knows you appreciate them. Say it. Every day.

Strategy 3: Create New Traditions

Empty nest, retirement, aging—each life stage allows new traditions. Morning walks, weekly date nights, annual trips, Sunday family dinners. Build traditions that create meaning.

Strategy 4: Stay Connected to Family

Grandchildren, adult children, extended family—these relationships enrich your later years. Invest in them.

Strategy 5: Serve Others

Retirement isn't just for self-indulgence. Serve your community, mentor young people, volunteer, and use your wisdom and experience to help others.

Strategy 6: Maintain Your Health

You can't control everything about aging, but you can:
- Exercise regularly (even gentle exercise matters)
- Eat well
- Take medications as prescribed
- Attend medical appointments
- Don't smoke or drink excessively
- Stay mentally active
- Maintain social connections

Strategy 7: Keep Learning and Growing

Don't become stagnant. Read, learn new skills, try new experiences, stay curious. Aging doesn't mean stopping growth.

Strategy 8: Plan Adventures While You Can

That trip you've dreamed of? Take it now. Physical capability declines. "Someday" becomes "too late" faster than you think.

Strategy 9: Forgive and Let Go

At this stage of life, holding grudges is exhausting and pointless. Forgive—your spouse, your family, yourself. Let go of bitterness. Life is too short.

Strategy 10: Love Generously

You've learned what matters. Love your spouse, your family, and your friends generously. Don't hold back expressions of love waiting for "the right moment." Every moment is the right moment.

What I've Learned at 63

I'm in the early stages of aging, but I've learned: From my first marriage: Don't waste decades with the wrong person. Life is too short for sustained unhappiness. From my divorce: It's never too late to change course and pursue happiness. From my second marriage: When you get it right, aging together is a gift. My wife and I take Sunday walks together, cook together, talk, laugh, and enjoy simple companionship. This is what the later years should look like.

From my parents: I watched my mother age and eventually die. I watched how health decline affects everything. I learned the importance of expressing love while you can. From my survey research: Long-term happy marriages share common traits—the couples communicate well, forgive readily, appreciate each other, they adapt together, and they prioritize companionship.

From couples married 50+ years: The secret isn't passion (though that's nice)—it's friendship, respect, shared history, and choosing each other again and again through all life's changes.

Reflection & Assessment

Personal Reflection
Who are we becoming together over time?
Are we growing companions or distant partners?
Partner Dialogue
What kind of partnership do we want in later years?
Reality Check
☐ Companionship
☐ Co-existence

The Bottom Line on Aging in Marriage

Growing old isn't easy. Bodies fail. Health declines. Friends die. Capabilities decrease. These are realities of aging, married or single. But aging with a loving partner who knows, understands, appreciates, and chooses you—that transforms the experience. The goal isn't to avoid aging or its challenges. That's impossible.

If you're young: Choose your partner wisely now, because you'll grow old together (hopefully). Build a relationship that can weather decades and all life's changes.

If you're middle-aged: Don't neglect your marriage amid work and parenting chaos. Invest now in the relationship that will sustain you in retirement.

If you're approaching retirement: Discuss your vision together. Plan financially, emotionally, and relationally. Prepare for this new phase.

If you're already retired: Make the most of every day. Express love freely. Create joy where you can. Handle challenges together. Treasure your time.

If you're dealing with serious health issues, show love through caregiving or through receiving care gracefully. Find moments of connection amid difficulty. Hold on to each other.

The years pass faster than you imagine. Don't waste them. Build a marriage that sustains you through every stage—young love, busy middle years, and quiet later years.

And when the end comes—as it will for all of us—may you be able to say: "We lived well. We loved well. We made the most of our time together."

That's the goal. That's success.

CHAPTER 21: LEGACY

The greatest inheritance you leave your children is not wealth
— it is the model of love they witnessed.

What We Leave Behind.

This is the final chapter—not just of this book, but the chapter we're all writing with our lives: What legacy will we leave? I think about legacy often. What am I leaving to the next generation? What did my first marriage teach my children? What does my second marriage model for them?

Legacy isn't just about what you accumulate—money, property, achievements. It's about what you impart—values, wisdom, examples, love, lessons.

This chapter is about the legacy your relationship creates—for your children, your family, your community, and the world.

What is Relational Legacy?

Relational legacy is the impact your relationship has on others, particularly the next generation.

Your relationship teaches others:
- What marriage can be
- How partners should treat each other
- What love looks like in action
- How to handle conflict
- How to stay committed
- When to stay and when to leave
- What partnership means
- How families function

You're modelling a relationship for:
- Your children
- Your grandchildren
- Your extended family
- Your friends and community
- Everyone who observes your relationship

Whether you intend to or not, you're teaching. The question is: What are you teaching?

My Children's Legacy From My First Marriage

Let me be honest about what my first marriage taught my four children:

What they learned (unintentionally):

- That you can stay in an unhappy marriage for decades
- That financial security sometimes outweighs emotional fulfilment
- That spouses can live together while barely communicating
- That cultural and religious expectations can trap you
- That you can love your children while being unhappy in your marriage
- That sacrifice—even misguided sacrifice—is sometimes valued

What I hope they also learned:

- That compatibility matters—choose carefully
- That communication is essential—we failed at it
- That education level affects marital dynamics
- That getting to know someone before marriage is crucial
- That cultural expectations shouldn't override personal happiness
- That staying "for the children" isn't always the right choice

What my divorce taught them:

- That it's never too late to choose happiness
- That mistakes can be corrected, even after decades
- That both parents can be okay after divorce
- That they weren't responsible for keeping us together
- That ending an unhappy marriage isn't failure—sometimes it's wisdom
- That second chances exist

What my second marriage is teaching them:

- What a healthy relationship looks like
- That genuine companionship is possible
- That marriage can be joyful, not just endured
- That communication makes everything easier
- That compatibility matters enormously
- That love can happen again at any age

My four children are all watching my second marriage. They see the difference. They see me happy. They see a healthy partnership modelled for the first time. I can't undo the years of unhappy marriage they witnessed. But I can show them now what marriage should look like. That's part of my legacy to them.

What Are You Teaching Your Children About Marriage?

If you have children, they're learning about relationships by observing yours. What are they learning?

Consider:

How do you speak to each other?
- With respect or contempt?
- With kindness or criticism?
- With patience or irritation?

Your children are noticing. They'll likely replicate these patterns in their relationships.

How do you handle conflict?
- With healthy communication or destructive fighting?
- With resolution or ongoing bitterness?
- With forgiveness or grudge-holding?

Your children are learning conflict resolution by watching you.

How do you show affection?
- Do you hug, kiss, hold hands?
- Do you express love verbally?
- Do you demonstrate appreciation?

Your children are learning how to express love by observing you.

How do you prioritize your marriage?
- Do you maintain date nights despite busy schedules?
- Do you support each other publicly?
- Do you work on your relationship intentionally?

Your children are learning what marriage priority looks like.

How do you handle stress?
- Do you support each other or blame each other?
- Do you face challenges together or separately?
- Do you maintain connection during difficult seasons?

Your children are learning how partners navigate life's challenges.

How do you share responsibilities?
- Do you work as a team?
- Do you respect each other's contributions?
- Do you communicate about household and childcare tasks?

Your children are learning about partnership and fairness.

What you model becomes their normal. If you model healthy relationships, they'll seek healthy relationships. If you model dysfunction, they may unknowingly replicate it.

This is an enormous responsibility. It's also a tremendous opportunity.

Legacy Through Divorce

Some of you worry that divorce has destroyed the legacy you hoped to leave your children. Let me address this.

Divorce does teach your children things:
- That some marriages don't work (this is realistic, not damaging)
- That people make mistakes in partner selection
- That it's possible to correct course even when painful
- That both parents can move forward healthily
- That they're not responsible for parental happiness

Divorce doesn't automatically harm children IF:
- You don't use children as weapons against each other
- You don't force children to choose sides
- You maintain respect when discussing the other parent
- You both continue loving and supporting the children
- You show them healthy relationships moving forward
- You take responsibility for your choices
- You let them maintain relationships with both parents

My children from my divorced first marriage:
- Have relationships with both their mother and me
- Understand that their mother and I were incompatible
- Don't blame themselves for our divorce
- Are not traumatized by our separation
- Are, in fact, healthier seeing me happy now

The legacy question after divorce: What will you do now? Will you become bitter or will you grow? Will you repeat patterns or learn from mistakes? Will you model resilience and healing or victimhood and blame? Your post-divorce behaviour teaches your children as much as the divorce itself.

Legacy Through Your Values

Beyond modelling relationship dynamics, you're passing on values. What values does your relationship demonstrate?

Consider what your marriage models about:

Commitment:
- Do you keep promises?
- Do you work through difficulties rather than quit easily?

- Do you honour your vows?

Respect:
- Do you value each other's opinions?
- Do you honour each other's boundaries?
- Do you treat each other with dignity?

Kindness:
- Do you show compassion during struggles?
- Do you help each other without keeping score?
- Do you speak gently even when frustrated?

Forgiveness:
- Do you hold grudges or let go?
- Do you apologize when wrong?
- Do you grant grace for mistakes?

Communication:
- Do you talk through problems?
- Do you listen actively?
- Do you express needs clearly?

Teamwork:
- Do you support each other's goals?
- Do you share responsibilities fairly?
- Do you make decisions together?

Faith (if applicable):
- Do you practice your faith genuinely?
- Does your faith strengthen your marriage?
- Do you model authentic spirituality?

Growth:
- Do you keep learning and improving?
- Do you acknowledge mistakes and change?
- Do you help each other become better?

These values—demonstrated daily in your marriage—become your children's inheritance.

Legacy To Grandchildren

If you're fortunate enough to have grandchildren, you have the opportunity to impact another generation.

What grandparents model:

Enduring love:

Seeing grandparents who still hold hands, still laugh together, still enjoy each other after 40+ years teaches grandchildren that lasting love is real.

Aging with grace:

How you handle aging—physical limitations, health challenges, loss—teaches grandchildren about resilience and acceptance.

Family importance:

Prioritizing family time, creating traditions, and staying connected teaches grandchildren that family matters.

Generational wisdom:

Sharing stories, passing on knowledge, and offering guidance connects generations and pass on wisdom.

Unconditional love:

Loving grandchildren freely teaches them they're valued simply for existing, not for achieving. I have four grandchildren—two boys, two girls.

What do I want them to learn from observing my marriage?

- That their grandfather chose happiness over obligation
- That genuine companionship is possible at any age
- That communication and respect are foundational
- That second chances are real
- That family bonds transcend divorce
- That love can be joyful, not just dutiful

That's the legacy I'm building for them now.

Legacy to Your Community

Your relationship impacts more than just your family.

You're modelling a relationship for:

- Friends observing your marriage
- Colleagues who know you
- Your religious community
- Younger couples seeking examples
- Anyone who interacts with you as a couple

Consider:

Do you model healthy relationships publicly?

- How you speak about your spouse to others
- How you interact at social gatherings
- How you support each other publicly
- How you handle disagreement when others are present

Do you support other couples?

- Through mentoring younger couples
- Through being honest about your own struggles
- Through celebrating others' marriages
- Through helping couples in crisis

Do you contribute to a healthy relationship culture?

- By refusing to participate in spouse-bashing

• By protecting your marriage's privacy while being appropriately transparent
• By promoting healthy relationship values
• By challenging unhealthy cultural norms

I currently mentor younger couples. I share my mistakes and successes. I model that marriage takes work, but that work is worth it. I want my legacy to include the marriages I helped strengthen.

What Legacy Do You Want To Leave?

Let me ask you directly: When you're gone, what do you want your children/grandchildren to say about your marriage?
• "They loved each other deeply."
• "They treated each other with respect."
• "They worked through everything together."
• "They showed us what partnership looks like."
• "They never gave up on each other."
• "They made marriage look joyful."
• "They taught us what matters."
Or will they say:
• "They stayed together but weren't happy."
• "They barely spoke to each other."
• "They modelled dysfunction."
• "They taught us to endure rather than thrive."
• "They should have divorced years earlier."
• "They showed us what not to do."

What legacy are you building? Today. Right now. Through your actions.

Practical Steps to Build The Legacy You Want

Step 1: Define Your Desired Legacy

Write down specifically what you want your marriage to teach and demonstrate. Be concrete. Not "be loving" but "demonstrate love through daily appreciation, physical affection, and supporting each other's dreams."

Step 2: Assess Your Current Reality

Honestly evaluate: Is your current marriage modelling what you want to teach? Where are you succeeding? Where are you failing?

Step 3: Identify Gaps

What's the difference between your desired legacy and your current reality? Work on closing the gaps.

Step 4: Create Specific Changes

For each gap, determine specific actions to close it. Not "communicate better" but "have 15-minute check-in conversations every evening without phones."

Step 5: Implement Consistently

Legacy is built through daily actions over the years. Implement your changes consistently, not sporadically.

Step 6: Model Publicly

Don't just improve privately. Model a healthy marriage publicly so others can learn from you.

Step 7: Teach Explicitly

Don't just model—also teach. Talk with your children about healthy relationships. Share what you've learned. Don't assume they'll figure it out by assimilation.

Step 8: Course-Correct

When you fail (you will), acknowledge it, apologize, and correct. Teaching how to handle failure is also a valuable legacy.

Step 9: Seek Help

If you can't build the legacy you want alone, get counselling. Seeking help models that problems can be solved and that asking for help is a strength.

Step 10: Stay Committed to the Vision

Building a legacy takes decades. Stay committed. Don't give up when it's hard.

Legacy Beyond Your Lifetime

True legacy extends beyond your life. What you teach your children, they'll teach their children. What you model for grandchildren shapes how they'll relate to their future spouses. You're not just affecting this generation—you're affecting multiple generations to come.

Consider:

Your great-grandchildren (who you may never meet) will be influenced by what you teach your grandchildren today. Your children's marriages will reflect what they learned observing yours. Your community will be shaped by whether you built a healthy or an unhealthy relationship culture. This is a profound responsibility. It's also tremendous opportunity.

The Legacy of This Book

Why did I write this book? Why share my failures, my divorce, my personal struggles? Because legacy isn't just personal—it's communal. If sharing this helps even one person:
- Choose more wisely at the beginning
- Leave an unhappy marriage sooner rather than waste decades
- Believe second chances are possible
- Build better relationships
- Model healthier partnerships for their children
- Learn from my mistakes rather than repeat them

Then my failures become valuable. Then my pain has purpose. Then my story becomes legacy. That's why I've been so transparent in this book. That's why I've shared statistics alongside personal stories. That's why I've been honest about what worked and what failed.

My legacy through this book: Help others build better relationships than I did the first time. Help people avoid my mistakes. Help those in failing marriages have the courage to act. Help divorced people believe happiness is possible again. If this book helps you—if you build better a relationship, if you leave destructive one, if you find love again, if you a model healthy partnership for your children—then I've left a legacy beyond my own family.

Reflection & Assessment

Personal Reflection
What relational example am I modelling?
What legacy am I intentionally building?
Partner Dialogue
What do we want others to learn from our relationship?
Reality Check
☐ Intentional legacy
☐ Unexamined legacy

Final Words On Legacy

Legacy isn't about perfection. I've proven you can fail spectacularly and still leave a positive a legacy if you learn, grow, and share what you've learned. Legacy isn't about never making mistakes. It's about learning from mistakes and helping others avoid them. Legacy isn't about always getting it right. It's about correcting course when you get it wrong.

Legacy is about:
- Living with integrity
- Loving generously
- Learning continuously
- Teaching honestly
- Modelling authentically
- Impacting positively
- Contributing meaningfully
- Leaving the world better than you found it

Your marriage—whether current, past, or future—is part of your legacy. Make it count. Treat your spouse with respect and kindness. Communicate openly. Work through problems. Stay committed when you should. Have the courage to leave when you must. Learn from failures. Build on successes. Model a healthy relationship. Teach the next generation. Leave a legacy of love. That's what I'm working toward in my second marriage. That's what I hope for you. That's what the world needs.

Build relationships worth modelling.

Leave a legacy worth having.

Live and love well.

Scan this code for a short reflection related to Part VI & VII.

THE SECOND BRIDGE

Appendices, Resources, and Additional Materials

APPENDIX A: SURVEY METHODOLOGY

1. DEMOGRAPHIC PROFILE OF RESPONDENT

The December 2018 – January 2019 survey combined responses from Africa, the USA, and interview-based qualitative data, resulting in more than 225 participants providing insight into modern relationship dynamics.

1.1 Gender Distribution

Across both major surveys (Africa + USA), the gender distribution was balanced, enabling representative comparison across cultures.

• Male: 117 (52%)

• Female: 107 (47%)

• Other/Unspecified: <1%

Region	Male	Female	Other / Unspecified
Africa	55 (61.8%)	33 (37%)	1 (1.2%)
USA	62 (45.3%)	74 (54.0%)	1 (0.7%)
Combined	117 (52%)	107 (47.6%)	2 (<1%)

Both surveys were fairly balanced, allowing meaningful comparison of gender perspectives.

1.2 Age Distribution
Africa Survey

Age Group	Count	Percent
18–24	11	12.3%
25–34	28	31.5%
35–44	20	22.5%
45–64	30	33.7%

USA Survey

(USA survey contained age bands from 18–29 up to 60+; detailed breakdown available if needed.)

The African dataset skewed slightly older, with the largest group

being ages 45–64, while the USA dataset leaned more
toward younger, digital-surveying adults.

1.3 Marital & Family Status (Africa Survey)

• Marital Status
• Single: 33%
• Married: 60%
• Divorced/Widowed: 7%
• Single Parents
• Yes: 18%
• No: 82%

A majority of respondents were in established relationships,
providing

strong relational insight for this book.

2. RELATIONSHIP CONSIDERATION FACTORS

Respondents were asked how important various characteristics
were when choosing a partner.

2.1 Importance Ratings (Africa Survey)

These were measured on a Likert scale (Strongly Agree → Strongly
Disagree).

Factor Considered	% of Respondents Agreeing It's Important
Height	28%
Beauty / Physical	63%
Level of Education	71%
Race	12%
Religion	68%
Age Difference	44%
Status / Social Standing	39%
Financial Stability	74%
Family Background	62%

Across cultures, education, finance, religion, and family
Background were consistently ranked as highly important.

3. EMOTIONAL AND RELATIONAL HEALTH INDICATORS

3.1 Trust in Partner (Africa Survey)

• Yes: 79%
• No: 21%

3.2 Happiness Level in Relationship

- Happy / Very Happy: 72%
- Unhappy / Indifferent: 28%

3.3 Would They Walk Away If They Had the Option?

- Yes: 34%
- No: 66%

Common reasons given for staying despite dissatisfaction:

- Children and family stability
- Financial dependence
- Cultural expectations
- Hope for change

A significant proportion remain in strained relationships for reasons not rooted in emotional fulfilment—a recurring theme in The Second Bridge.

4. CULTURAL DIFFERENCES: USA VS AFRICA

4.1 Relationship Priorities

USA respondents placed relatively higher value on:

- Personal happiness
- Emotional connection
- Shared interests
- Mental health compatibility

Africa respondents emphasised:

- Religion
- Family background
- Financial readiness

4.2 Regional Trends in Walking Away

USA respondents expressed:

- More willingness to walk away if unhappy
- Higher emphasis on self-actualisation in relationships

Africa respondents showed:

- Greater reluctance due to cultural obligations
- Stronger influence of family systems

5. QUALITATIVE INSIGHTS (THEMATIC ANALYSIS)

From interview comments and open-ended survey responses, several themes emerged:

Positive Relationship Drivers

- Kindness, loyalty & support
- Communication & understanding
- Shared values (especially faith)

Negative Relationship Drivers

- Financial strain
- Lack of communication

• Trust issues
• Family interference
• Emotional neglect
Universal Themes Across Cultures
• People deeply desire love, safety, and partnership
• Many struggle with expectations vs reality
• A notable number remain in relationships due to fear, children, cultural constraints, or finances
These themes inform many of the book's core messages.

6. SUMMARY STATISTICAL HIGHLIGHTS FOR THE APPENDIX

• Over 225 respondents participated across Africa, USA, and interview datasets.
• 48% male, 52% female, <1% non-binary/unspecified.
• Most common age group: 25–44 across both data sets.
• Education (71%), finance (74%), religion (68%), and family background (62%) are the strongest relationship consideration factors.
• 72% of partnered respondents described themselves as happy.
• 34% would leave their relationship if they had the option—suggesting emotional dissatisfaction beneath cultural expectations.
• Cultural differences strongly influenced relationship expectations:
• USA: Emotional fulfilment & autonomy
• Africa: Stability, religion, and family systems
African Sample Profile (n=84)
Gender: 62% Male, 37% Female
Marital Status: 61% Married, 37% Single, 1% Divorced, 1% Widowed Age
Distribution: 35% ages 45-64, 31% ages 25-34, 21% ages 35-44, 13% ages 18-24
Religion: 77% Christian, 17% Muslim, 3% Atheist, 3% Other/Traditional
Employment: 71% Employed, 13% Students, 8% Unemployed, 7% Retired
Countries: Kenya (37%), Nigeria (14%), Uganda (10%), South Africa (10%), Ghana (4%), Other African nations (25%)
Single Parents: 25%
USA Sample Profile (n=136)
Gender: 54% Female, 46% Male

Marital Status: 54% Married, 31% Single, 12% Divorced, 3% Widowed

Age Distribution: 51% ages 35-44, 20% ages 55-64, 18% ages 18-24, 9% ages 65+

Religion: 65% Christian, 20% Other, 9% Atheist, 3% Traditional, 2% Hindu, 1% Muslim

Employment: 64% Employed, 14% Unemployed, 14% Retired, 7% Students

Geographic Distribution: South Atlantic (21%), East North Central (20%), Middle Atlantic (18%), West South Central (14%), other regions

Household Income: Most common brackets: $25,000-$49,999 (23%), $50,000-$74,999 (19%), $100,000-$124,999 (13%)

Single Parents: 18%

Survey Methodology Notes

Both surveys used similar question structures to enable cross-cultural comparison

Likert scale responses (Strongly Disagree to Strongly Agree) used for factor importance

Role importance measured on 5-point scale (Not at all important to Extremely important)

Open-ended questions captured qualitative insights about partner qualities and relationship concerns

Total combined sample: 225 respondents

Data collection period: December 2018 & January 2019

Respondents completed a 17 (USA) 19 (Africa)-question survey addressing:

- Factors in partner selection
- Reasons for entering marriage
- Importance of finance, religion, communication
- Sources of marital conflict
- Conflict resolution approaches
- Satisfaction with various relationship elements
- Cultural influences on relationship expectations

RESEARCH ETHICS

All participants provided informed consent. Identifying information has been changed in interview excerpts to protect privacy. The research was conducted with cultural sensitivity and respect for diverse perspectives and practices.

APPENDIX B: INTERVIEW INSIGHTS AND COMMON THEMES

INTERVIEW METHODOLOGY

In addition to the 220 quantitative survey, we conducted in-depth interviews with 4 couples and 1 individual across multiple countries. These interviews lasted 45-90 minutes and explored relationship experiences in greater depth than the survey allowed and the outcome form part of Appendix A.

Relationships

• Family obligations, cultural norms, and religious beliefs frequently prevent people from leaving.

• Financial dependency and the presence of children reinforce commitment even when emotional needs are unmet.

• Fear of judgment or shame is a recurring barrier to separation.

Cultural Insights

• USA respondents prioritise personal happiness, communication, and autonomy.

• African respondents emphasise duty, family cohesion, and religious alignment.

• Each culture defines 'relationship success' in distinct ways.

Love, Expectations & Reality

• Many respondents reported tension between the reality of their relationship and the expectations they entered with.

• Both regions expressed that love alone is insufficient without communication skills and emotional literacy.

APPENDIX C: AUTHOR'S PERSONAL REFLECTIONS AND LESSONS LEARNED

INTRODUCTION

This book represents more than research and observation—it represents my lived experience, including both profound failures and hard-won successes. In this appendix, I want to share some personal reflections that didn't fit neatly into the main chapters but that continue to shape how I understand relationships, marriage, and love. These reflections are offered with humility. I don't claim to have mastered marriage. But failure, I've learned, can be as instructive as success. Perhaps more so.

WHAT GROWING UP POLYGAMOUS TAUGHT ME

What I learned:

- Love is not a finite resource—my father loved all his children
- Resources, however, are finite—there was never enough attention, time, or money
- Competition for affection damages children and relationships
- Women in polygamous arrangements often suffer silently
- Children become caretakers of their mothers' emotional needs
- Jealousy is inevitable when people must share what should be exclusive
- Family structure profoundly shapes what you believe is possible

When I chose monogamy, I wasn't rejecting my father or my culture. I was choosing a different path based on what I witnessed growing up. I wanted my wife to never wonder if she had my full heart. I wanted my children to never compete for my attention with siblings from other mothers.

But I also carry deep respect for my father and my mothers. They did the best they could within their cultural context. Their sacrifices gave me opportunities they never had.

WHAT MY FIRST MARRIAGE TAUGHT ME

In the early years, I believed love could overcome anything. I thought working harder, praying more, and being more patient would fix what was broken. I believed divorce was failure, and I was terrified of failing.

In the middle years, I stayed for my children. I didn't want them to experience divorce. I wanted to give them stability, even if it meant my own unhappiness. Looking back, I realize they knew we were unhappy. My sacrifice didn't protect them—it taught them that misery is normal in marriage.

In the later years, I stayed because leaving seemed impossible. We had built a life together—shared finances, shared friends, shared history. Starting over at 50, then 55, then 60 seemed overwhelming. The known misery felt safer than unknown possibility. What finally changed? I reached a point where staying was killing my spirit more than leaving would hurt anything else. At 61 years old, I decided I wanted to know what joy felt like before I died. That decision changed everything.

What my first marriage taught me:
- Love alone is not enough to sustain marriage
- You cannot change another person—they must want to change
- Children know when parents are unhappy, even when you hide it
- Staying in a bad marriage "for the kids" can harm them as much as divorce
- Resentment accumulates over years and becomes toxic
- Some relationships cannot be saved, no matter how hard you try
- There is no shame in admitting you made a mistake
- Divorce is not failure—sometimes it is the courageous choice

WHAT DIVORCE TAUGHT ME

It was the most painful and liberating experience of my life.
The pain:
- Grieving not just the loss of a person, but the loss of who I thought I'd be
- Telling my children that their parents were divorcing devastated me
- Dividing a life built over decades felt like tearing myself in half
- Facing judgment from family, friends, and community
- Questioning every decision I'd made for nearly four decades
- Starting a new relationship all over again
- Loneliness in the beginning was overwhelming
The liberation:
- Freedom from walking on eggshells every day
- Relief from constant tension and conflict
- Rediscovering who I am outside of an unhappy marriage
- Realizing I could still build a good life at 61
- Learning that endings can be beginnings

• Discovering that joy was still possible for me
• Understanding that I deserved happiness too
What divorce taught me:
• Sometimes the most loving thing you can do is let go
• Divorce doesn't mean the marriage was meaningless—we had good years and raised wonderful children
• Failure teaches lessons that success never could
• Starting over at any age is possible
• My children are more resilient than I gave them credit for
• Self-compassion is essential—I was doing the best I could with what I knew
• Other people's opinions matter less than your own peace

WHAT MY SECOND MARRIAGE IS TEACHING ME

My current wife brings joy, wisdom, and partnership to my life in ways I never experienced before. This marriage is different because:
• I chose her with wisdom, not just passion
• I know who I am now—I didn't know at 25
• I communicate openly because I've seen what silence destroys
• I address problems immediately instead of letting them fester
• I appreciate the small things because I know relationships are fragile
• I choose love daily—it's a verb, not just a feeling
• I'm a better partner because I learned from failing before
What my second marriage is teaching me:
• It's never too late to find love and partnership
• The right relationship shouldn't require constant work to survive
• Peace in a relationship is not boring—it's beautiful
• Compatibility matters as much as chemistry
• A good partner celebrates your growth instead of fearing it
• You can have both independence and intimacy
• Second chances are real
• Love in your 60s is different from love in your 20s—and that's wonderful

LESSONS I WISH I'D LEARNED EARLIER

If I could go back and talk to my 25-year-old self on his wedding day, here's what I would say:

1. Choose your partner wisely—passion fades, character remains. Marry someone whose character you admire.

2. Learn to communicate before you marry—most marital problems stem from communication failures. Get counselling before you need it.

3. Discuss everything before marriage—money, children, roles, expectations, family, religion. Assumptions destroy relationships.

4. Address problems immediately—small resentments become large bitterness over time. Never let the sun set on your anger.

5. You cannot change another person—accept who they are or don't marry them. Hoping they'll change is setting yourself up for disappointment.

6. Maintain your identity—don't lose yourself in marriage. You can be "we" while still being "I."

7. Financial stress will test you—handle money wisely and communicate about it openly. Many marriages die over money.

8. Children complicate but don't fix—don't have children to save a marriage. They will magnify whatever is already there.

9. Physical intimacy requires emotional intimacy—sex problems are usually relationship problems. Work on connection.

10. Seek help early—counselling is not for failures, it's for wise people who want to succeed. Get help before crisis.

11. It's okay to admit you made a mistake—staying in a bad marriage doesn't make you noble, it makes you stuck. Sometimes divorce is the right choice.

12. You deserve happiness too—self-sacrifice sounds noble, but martyrdom helps no one. Your wellbeing matters.

FINAL REFLECTION

I am now 63 years old. I have been married twice. I have four adult children and several grandchildren. I have lived in three countries. I have experienced both profound failure and unexpected joy in relationships.

If there's one thing I've learned, it's this: Love is both simpler and more complex than we think. Simpler because it comes down to daily choices—to listen, to appreciate, to forgive, to try again. More complex because every person brings a lifetime of experiences, wounds, hopes, and fears into relationship. Navigating two complex humans building one life together requires patience, humility, wisdom, and grace.

This book represents my attempt to share what 225 respondents and two very different marriages have taught me about building lasting love. I hope it helps you build bridges—across cultural differences, relationship challenges, past failures, and future hopes.

Thank you for reading.

May you build well.

APPENDIX D: ADDITIONAL RESOURCES

RECOMMENDED BOOKS
Relationship Communication
- "Hold Me Tight" by Dr. Sue Johnson
- "The Seven Principles for Making Marriage Work" by John Gottman
- "Crucial Conversations" by Kerry Patterson et al.
- "Nonviolent Communication" by Marshall Rosenberg

Financial Partnership
- "The Total Money Makeover" by Dave Ramsey
- "Smart Couples Finish Rich" by David Bach
- "Your Money or Your Life" by Vicki Robin and Joe Dominguez

Cross-Cultural Relationships
- "The Culture Map" by Erin Meyer
- "Intercultural Marriage" by Dugan Romano
- "Cross-Cultural Connections" by Duane Elmer

Marriage Enrichment
- "The Meaning of Marriage" by Timothy Keller
- "The 5 Love Languages" by Gary Chapman
- "Getting the Love You Want" by Harville Hendrix

Divorce and Healing
- "Rebuilding" by Bruce Fisher
- "Spiritual Divorce" by Debbie Ford
- "The Good Divorce" by Constance Ahrons

PROFESSIONAL ORGANIZATIONS
Marriage and Family Therapy
American Association for Marriage and Family Therapy (AAMFT)
Website: www.aamft.org
Find a therapist: www.aamft.org/Directories

Counselling
American Counselling Association (ACA)
Website: www.Counselling.org
Counselling Association of South Africa (CASA)
Website: www.counselling-sa.co.za

Financial Counselling
National Foundation for Credit Counselling (NFCC)

Website: www.nfcc.org

National Credit Regulator (NCR), Website: www.ncr.org.za

Cross-Cultural Support

Families in Global Transition, Website: www.figt.org

South African Federation for Mental Health (SAFMH) Website: www.safmh.org

ONLINE RESOURCES

Marriage Education

- The Gottman Institute: www.gottman.com
- Prepare/Enrich: www.prepare-enrich.com
- National Marriage Project: www.nationalmarriageproject.org

Financial Tools

- Mint (budgeting app): www.mint.com
- You Need a Budget (YNAB): www.youneedabudget.com
- Smart About Money: www.smartaboutmoney.org

Communication Tools

- Couples app: www.couplesby.app
- Lasting app: www.getlasting.com
- Relish app: www.getrelish.com

ASSESSMENT TOOLS

- The Couple Agreement Audit: www.thesecondbridgebook.com
- The Gottman Relationship Check-up: www.gottman.com
- Myers-Briggs Type Indicator (MBTI)
- The 5 Love Languages Assessment: www.5lovelanguages.com
- Financial Personality Assessment: www.moneyhabitudes.com

RETREAT AND ENRICHMENT PROGRAMS

- Marriage Encounter Weekend
- Couple Communication Program
- The Art and Science of Love Workshop (Gottman Method)
- Retrouvaille (for couples in crisis)
- Marriage Alive Seminars

AUTHOR'S WEBSITE

For additional resources, updates, and to connect with the author:
Website: www.thesecondbridgebook.com
Email: info@rdc.global
Blog: https://blog.thesecondbridgebook.com
Newsletter: Sign up for monthly relationship insights and practical tips at https://blog.thesecondbridgebook.com

THE SECOND BRIDGE

APPENDIX E: BRIDGING WESTERN AND AFRICAN RELATIONAL FRAMEWORKS

Individual fulfilment → Communal responsibility and shared purpose

Personal boundaries → Relational accountability within community

Couple-centric intimacy → Family-embedded intimacy

Conflict resolution → Restorative harmony and mediation

Emotional independence → Interdependence and mutual care

Resilience as endurance → Resilience with voice, dignity, and repair

BIBLIOGRAPHY: BOOKS CONSULTED

• Chapman, Gary. The 5 Love Languages: The Secret to Love that Lasts. Northfield Publishing, 2015.

• Gottman, John M., and Nan Silver. The Seven Principles for Making Marriage Work. Harmony Books, 2015.

• Johnson, Sue. Hold Me Tight: Seven Conversations for a Lifetime of Love. Little, Brown and Company, 2008.

• Keller, Timothy. The Meaning of Marriage: Facing the Complexities of Commitment with the Wisdom of God. Penguin Books, 2011.

• Patterson, Kerry, et al. Crucial Conversations: Tools for Talking When Stakes Are High. McGraw-Hill Education, 2011.

• Perel, Esther. Mating in Captivity: Unlocking Erotic Intelligence. Harper Paperbacks, 2007.

• Romano, Dugan. Intercultural Marriage: Promises and Pitfalls. Intercultural Press, 2008.

Emecheta, Buchi. The Joys of Motherhood. George Braziller, 1979.

Oyěwùmí, Oyèrónkẹ́. The Invention of Women: Making an African Sense of Western Gender Discourses. University of Minnesota Press, 1997.

Sekyiamah, Nana Darkoa. The Sex Lives of Africa Women. HarperCollins, 2022.

Somé, Sobonfu. The Spirit of Intimacy: Ancient African Teachings in the Ways of Relationships. HarperOne, 1999

wa Thiong'o, Ngũgĩ. Decolonising the Mind: The Politics of Language in African Literature. Heinemann, 1986

RESEARCH ARTICLES AND STUDIES

• Amato, Paul R. "Research on Divorce: Continuing Trends and New Developments." Journal of Marriage and Family 72, no. 3 (2010): 650-666.

• Bramlett, Matthew D., and William D. Mosher. "Cohabitation, Marriage, Divorce, and Remarriage in the United States." National Center for Health Statistics. Vital Health Statistics 23, no. 22 (2002).

• Fincham, Frank D., and Steven R.H. Beach. "Marriage in the New Millennium: A Decade in Review." Journal of Marriage and Family 72, no. 3 (2010): 630-649.

• Gottman, John M., and Robert W. Levenson. "The Timing of Divorce: Predicting When a Couple Will Divorce Over a 14-Year Period." Journal of Marriage and Family 62, no. 3 (2000): 737-745.

• Hetherington, E. M., & Kelly, J. (2002). For Better or For Worse: Divorce Reconsidered.

• Larson, J. (2002). Emotional intelligence and marital satisfaction. Journal of Family Issues.

• Markman, Howard J., et al. "The Premarital Communication Roots of Marital Distress and Divorce." Journal of Family Psychology 24, no. 3 (2010): 289-298.

• Stanley, Scott M., et al. "Premarital Education, Marital Quality, and Marital Stability." Journal of Family Psychology 20, no. 1 (2006): 117-126.

• Centers for Disease Control and Prevention. (2023). National marriage and divorce rate trends. National Center for Health Statistics.

• U.S. Census Bureau. (2023). America's families and living arrangements: 2023. Washington, DC: U.S. Census Bureau.

• Statistics South Africa. (2024). General household survey 2023. Pretoria: Statistics South Africa.

CULTURAL AND SOCIOLOGICAL REFERENCES

• Coontz, Stephanie. Marriage, a History: How Love Conquered Marriage. Penguin Books, 2006.

• Hofstede, Geert, et al. Cultures and Organizations: Software of the Mind. McGraw-Hill, 2010.

• Meyer, Erin. The Culture Map: Breaking Through the Invisible Boundaries of Global Business. Public Affairs, 2014.

Amadiume, Ifi. Male Daughters, Female Husbands: Gender and Sex in an African Society. Zed Books, 1987.

ONLINE RESOURCES

• American Association for Marriage and Family Therapy. www.aamft.org

• National Center for Health Statistics. www.cdc.gov/nchs

• Pew Research Center: Marriage and Divorce Statistics. www.pewresearch.org

• The Gottman Institute. www.gottman.com

• United Nations Department of Economic and Social Affairs: Marriage and Family Statistics. www.un.org/development/desa

SURVEYS AND DATA SOURCES

Original survey data collected by author (2018-2019):

•225 respondent (220 respondents from USA and African nations and 5 in-depth couple interviews)

• Survey methodology detailed in Appendix A

NOTE ON SOURCES

All research, statistics, and quotes in this book have been carefully documented and attributed. Where personal interviews provided information, identifying details have been changed to protect privacy while maintaining accuracy of experiences shared.

ABOUT THE RESEARCH: THE SURVEY

I conducted comprehensive research on relationships and marriage across two continents in 2018 & 2019. This research forms the foundation of the data-driven insights throughout this book.

Survey Scope:

• 225 total respondents

• 137 from the United States (60.9%)

• 88 from African nations (39.1%)

• Respondents aged 25-72

• Mixture of married, engaged, divorced, and single (previously married) individuals

Survey Method:

Respondents completed a 17 (USA) 19 (Africa)-question survey addressing:

• Factors in partner selection

• Reasons for entering marriage

• Importance of finance, religion, communication

• Sources of marital conflict

• Conflict resolution approaches

• Satisfaction with various relationship elements

• Cultural influences on relationship expectations

RESEARCH ETHICS

All participants provided informed consent. Identifying information has been changed in interview excerpts to protect privacy. The research was conducted with cultural sensitivity and respect for diverse perspectives and practices.

THE COUPLE AGREEMENT AUDIT

"Every relationship runs on agreements—the danger is when no one remembers agreeing." — The Second Bridge

INTRODUCTION

Your relationship is operating on a set of rules right now. Expectations about who does what, how you handle conflict, what commitment means, how you'll raise children, what success looks like.

But here's the truth most couples won't admit: Most of these "agreements" were never actually agreed upon.

They assembled themselves from assumptions, cultural norms, things your parents' relationships taught you, casual comments that became rules, and silence that got interpreted as consent.

This Agreement Audit brings those invisible agreements into the light. It's uncomfortable work. But it's the work that builds lasting love.

HOW TO USE THIS AUDIT
STEP 1: Individual Completion (30-45 minutes)

Each partner should complete this audit separately, without discussing answers beforehand. Be completely honest—this is not about giving the "right" answer, it's about revealing what you actually believe.

STEP 2: Compare Answers (60-90 minutes)

Sit down together and compare your responses question by question. The goal is not agreement on everything—it's awareness of where you differ and whether those differences are manageable.

STEP 3: Negotiate Explicit Agreements (Ongoing)

Where you discover misalignment, have the conversation you should have had years ago: "So what ARE we actually agreeing to here?"

STEP 4: Document Your Agreements

Write down what you agree to. Revisit these agreements annually or when major life changes occur.

SCORING YOUR ALIGNMENT

After completing the audit together:
- 40-50 aligned answers (80-100% alignment)

STRONG FOUNDATION

You've had the hard conversations. You know where you stand.
Keep communicating and renegotiating as life changes.
- 30-39 aligned answers (60-79% alignment)

MODERATE ALIGNMENT

You're on solid ground with important gaps to address. Schedule
dedicated time to discuss the misaligned areas before they
become problems.
- 20-29 aligned answers (40-59% alignment)

SIGNIFICANT MISALIGNMENT

You've been operating under different assumptions about major
relationship areas. You need serious, explicit conversations
about where you're building toward.
- Fewer than 20 aligned answers (below 40% alignment)

CRISIS TERRITORY

You're essentially running two different relationships. This
level of misalignment requires professional counselling to
navigate safely.

Remember: Disagreement isn't failure. It's information. The
couples who last aren't the ones who agree on everything—they're the
ones who know where they disagree and have explicit plans for
navigating those differences.

SECTION 1: HOUSEHOLD & DAILY LIFE

1. Who is primarily responsible for household management (planning meals, managing schedules, organizing the home)?

☐ Partner A

☐ Partner B

☐ Shared equally

☐ We've never discussed this

☐ Other: _______________________

Why this matters: One partner often ends up with the "mental load" without it ever being discussed. This invisible labour creates resentment.

2. How do we divide household chores?

☐ Based on who has more time

☐ Based on traditional gender roles

☐ Equal division regardless of other factors

☐ Whoever notices it needs doing does it

☐ We hire help

☐ We've never explicitly agreed

☐ Other: _______________________

3. How do we handle disagreements about cleanliness standards?

☐ We have similar standards

☐ One person's standards prevail

☐ We compromise in the middle

☐ We avoid discussing it

☐ We've never had this conversation

☐ Other: _______________________

Your specific agreement:

____

____

SECTION 2: FINANCES & MONEY

4. How do we make major financial decisions (buying a house, car, investments)?

☐ Joint decision—both must agree

☐ Whoever earns more decides

☐ Each partner handles their own finances

☐ We discuss but one person has final say

☐ We've never established a process

☐ Other: _________________

5. What is our agreement about individual spending without consulting each other?

Amount: $_________ per purchase or $_________ per month

☐ We've never set a number

☐ We have different numbers in our heads

☐ We don't need limits—we trust each other

☐ Other: _________________

6. How do we handle debt?

☐ No debt is acceptable

☐ Some debt (mortgage, education) is acceptable

☐ Each person responsible for their own debt

☐ Debt is a shared responsibility

☐ We've never discussed our philosophy

☐ Other: _________________

7. What are we saving for? (Check all that apply)

☐ Retirement

☐ House/property

☐ Children's education

☐ Emergencies

☐ Travel/experiences

☐ Not actively saving

☐ We have different priorities

☐ We've never aligned on this

8. If one partner wants to make a major career change that affects household income, what's our agreement?

☐ Both must agree

☐ Individual autonomy—each person decides their career

☐ Depends on financial impact

☐ We'd figure it out when it happens

☐ We've never discussed this scenario

☐ Other: _________________

Your specific financial agreements:

____

____

SECTION 3: TIME, SPACE & INDEPENDENCE

9. How much alone time is healthy for each of us?

Partner A needs: _________ hours/days per week

Partner B needs: _________ hours/days per week

☐ We've never quantified this

☐ We don't believe in needing "alone time"

☐ This changes based on life circumstances

10. What is our agreement about friendships outside the marriage?

☐ Both partners maintain separate friendships freely

☐ Opposite-sex friendships require transparency/boundaries

☐ Most socializing should be as a couple

☐ Friend time should not interfere with couple time

☐ We've never explicitly discussed this

☐ Other: _________________

11. How do we handle social obligations (work events, family gatherings, friend invitations)?

☐ We attend together unless impossible

☐ Each person can decline for both of us

☐ Each person represents themselves only

☐ Depends on whose obligation it is

☐ We've never had a system

☐ Other: _________________

12. What role do our extended families play in our daily life?

☐ Very involved (daily/weekly contact)

☐ Moderately involved (monthly contact)

☐ Limited involvement (holidays only)

☐ Minimal to no involvement

☐ We have different expectations about this

☐ Other: _________________

13. Where do we want to live long-term?

☐ Current city/country

☐ Near family

☐ Where career opportunities are best

☐ Where we can afford the lifestyle we want

☐ We haven't decided/agreed

☐ We want different things

☐ Other: _________________

Your specific agreements about time and space:

____

____

____

NOTE

This Word document contains the first 3 sections of the Agreement Audit. The complete audit includes 11 sections with 50 questions covering:

   ✓ Section 1: Household & Daily Life (Questions 1-3)

   ✓ Section 2: Finances & Money (Questions 4-8)

   ✓ Section 3: Time, Space & Independence (Questions 9-13)

   • Section 4: Communication & Conflict (Questions 14-17)

   • Section 5: Intimacy & Affection (Questions 18-21)

   • Section 6: Children & Parenting (Questions 22-33)

   • Section 7: Career & Ambition (Questions 34-36)

   • Section 8: Religion & Values (Questions 37-39)

   • Section 9: The Relationship Itself (Questions 40-45)

   • Section 10: The Hard Questions (Questions 46-50)

Plus detailed guidance on:
• Interpreting your results
• Conversation starters for difficult topics
• Action plans based on your alignment score
• Resources for further support

THE SECOND BRIDGE

To take the complete Couple Agreement Audit, scan the QR code below:

ABOUT THE AUTHOR

The author brings a unique and deeply personal perspective to the conversation about relationships, marriage, and family. Born and raised in Nigeria within a polygamous household, he experienced first-hand the complexities, richness, and challenges of traditional African family structures. This upbringing provided him with invaluable insights into the dynamics of extended families, multiple relationships under one roof, and the intricate web of cultural expectations that shape how we love and live together.

Through his own cross-cultural marriage and the over 35 years of experience of raising children, he gained practical wisdom that cannot be found in textbooks. Not content to rely solely on personal experience, he conducted comprehensive research surveying 225 respondents from both the United States and Africa. This research forms the empirical backbone of this book, providing data-driven insights into what really matters in relationships across cultures. The survey revealed surprising similarities and important differences in how couples on two continents view love, finance, religion, trust, and the fundamental building blocks of lasting partnerships.

As a professional who has worked in several countries across the world, he understands the practical challenges couples face in balancing career demands, cultural expectations, religious commitments, and the day-to-day realities of building a life together. His insights come not from ivory tower theories but from the trenches of real relationships, real conflicts, and real triumphs.

This book represents decades of observation, experience, research, and reflection. It is written with the humility of someone who has made mistakes and learned from them, the confidence of someone who has successfully navigated raising children and managing relationships, and the generosity of someone who wants to help others avoid the pitfalls while embracing the possibilities that cross-cultural relationships offer.

Whether you are planning to go into a relationship, preparing for marriage, strengthening an existing relationship, navigating cultural differences with your partner, or simply seeking to understand the universal principles that sustain love across continents and generations, the author's unique perspective offers something valuable. His voice is authentic, his research is solid, and his commitment to helping couples build strong, lasting relationships is evident on every page.

READER REFLECTIONS

Voices in Conversation with The Second Bridge
The reflections below came from early reader who engaged deeply with the themes and questions raised in this book. The voices do not speak for the author, but with him—naming what resonated, what challenged them, and what felt necessary in the context of African relationships and family life.

Professor Emmanuel Ojo

Deputy Head of School, Wits School of Education

The Second Bridge is a book that speaks quietly, but with weight. It does not posture as expert knowledge, nor does it rush to offer answers. Instead, it feels like a conversation one has later in life, after having seen enough to know that certainty is often earned through pain. As I read, I recognised something deeply familiar: the African experience of staying, enduring, adjusting, and carrying responsibility long after joy has thinned out.

The author does not write to impress. He writes because he has lived the consequences of unexamined assumptions about marriage, duty, faith, and masculinity. What stands out is his courage to assert that longevity alone is not virtue, and that survival within a relationship does not automatically translate into wholeness. This is not a rejection of commitment, but a call to honesty. In African contexts where marriage is often upheld as an unquestionable moral achievement, such reflection is both rare and necessary.

What makes this book resonate deeply is the way it surfaces inherited blind spots. Culture, family expectations, religion, and silence are not presented as enemies, but as powerful forces that must be named if they are not to quietly rule our lives. The idea of a "second bridge" is especially meaningful in an African sense. It is not about abandoning the past, but about recognising that the first crossing was shaped by what we did not yet understand.

The second bridge is built with awareness, intention, and the humility that comes from having failed without being destroyed. The book neither glorifies divorce nor shames it. Instead, it asks a harder and more necessary question: how do we live truthfully, relationally, and responsibly, especially when the cost of silence is the slow erosion of the soul? In that question, many African readers will find not judgement, but recognition.